THE GREAT COOKS' GUIDE TO

Cookery

America's leading food authorities share their home-tested recipes and expertise on cooking equipment and techniques

THE GREAT COOKS' GUIDE TO

Fish

Cookery

A BEARD GLASER WOLF BOOK

RANDOM HOUSE, NEW YORK

Book Design by Milton Glaser, Inc.

Cover Photograph by Richard Jeffery

Library of Congress Cataloguing in Publication Data
Main entry under title:
The Great cooks' guide to fish cookery.
(The Great cooks' library)
1. Cookery (Fish) I. Title: Fish cookery.
II. Series.
TX747.G77   641.6'92   77-5974
ISBN: 394-73424-6

Manufactured in the United States of America
2 4 6 8 9 7 5 3
First Edition

We have gathered together some of the great cooks in this country to share their recipes—and their expertise—with you. As you read the recipes, you will find that in certain cases techniques will vary. This is as it should be: cooking is a highly individual art, and our experts have arrived at their own personal methods through years of experience in the kitchen.

THE EDITORS

Contents

FISH

SHELLFISH

In the hands of an able cook, fish can become an inexhaustible source of perpetual delight.
                    J. A. Brillat-Savarin

Fish Cookery

What's your idea of the Typical American Meal? Steak, right? Or fried chicken? But never, never fish, because Americans just don't eat fish.

Wrong you are. Americans, as a matter of fact, eat a lot of fish. Yet somehow we don't think of fish as typically American food because we prepare it in so many ways that come from our various ethnic backgrounds. Outside of the perfect tuna fish sandwich, the ubiquitous shrimp cocktail in red sauce, what is American fish cookery, anyway?

Well, you might start with sweet lobsters pulled from the icy waters off Maine and plunged into boiling sea water on the beach. Or tiny clams, dipped in batter, fried, and served in hash-houses all over New England. Or thick swordfish steaks, broiled over charcoal; or hard-shelled crabs steamed with peppercorns and served with tankards of beer in a restaurant overlooking Chesapeake Bay. Oyster stew, oysters Rockefeller, and salt-kissed oysters opened by the dozen or half-dozen at a commuters' bar in New York City. *Cioppino*—a tomato-laden fish stew—in San Francisco; gumbo in New Orleans; trout taken from a stream in the Rockies and fried then-and-there for breakfast; mussels in tomato sauce redolent with garlic; salmon for Sunday brunch. When we are able to rattle off so many succulent dishes so easily, how did we get the idea that Americans don't like to prepare fish? These are all foods in the highest culinary tradition, made of perfect local ingredients.

The difficulty is with that word "local." Fish is perishable, so that traditionally it was cooked near its source. That means that if you live in New England, you have been brought up knowing how to cook lobster, but you may be reluctant to sauté a trout. If you are from the Midwest, you are familiar with the preparation of fresh water fish, but you hesitate to try your hand at soft-shelled crabs. Or you learned from your Italian mother how to make *ensalata pescatore,* a mélange of cold seafood with a tart oil-and-vinegar dressing, but you wouldn't dream of attempting baked bass with stuffed fruit. In fact, we are all familiar with our own small corners of the world of fish cookery, our regional and ethnic specialties. Modern techniques of preservation, however, have outpaced our skills, and whereas we can now fly the products of our waters all over the country within hours, we are still trying to learn the best ways of preparing them.

It's not hard at all. Fish is one of those foods that respond best to the minimum of fuss: the Japanese eat fish raw, for heaven's sake! A little attention at the time it is purchased, some care in its storage, and you can't go far wrong.

1

Canadian Fisheries Rule: And now, to make fish cookery even less chancy, we have a definitive rule on timing developed by the Canadian Fisheries and Marine Service. It will free you forever of concern about whether your fish will be undercooked or overcooked. The formula requires two things: a ruler and a clock.

This is it. Lay the fish on its side and measure it at its thickest point. *Then cook the fish for ten minutes for every inch of thickness. If the fish is frozen, double this time: that is, cook it for 20 minutes for every inch of thickness.* Needless to say, a half-inch-thick fish should be cooked for half the time—five minutes—while a half-inch-thick frozen fish should be cooked for 10 minutes. Refer to this rule whenever you are going to cook fish until you know it by heart. *Note:* When baking fish in an open dish, this rule applies *only* if the oven is preheated to 450 degrees and the fish is placed on the middle rack.

Buying Fish: Good fish cookery begins at the water's edge or at the market: unless you are catching your own, it pays to search out a reputable fishmonger, and to be adamant, absolutely unswervable, about freshness. You can tell a fish is fresh if the eyes are clear and bulging, the gills are bright red or pink, and the scales are tight against the body. Immaculately fresh fish has no odor at all, and its flesh feels firm to the touch. Lobsters and crabs should be purchased only when they are still alive, when you can see them moving. Mollusks—oysters, clams and mussels—must also be bought alive, with tightly closed shells. A tap on the shell of a slightly opened clam or oyster should cause it to close more tightly. Discard any shells that are cracked or partially opened.

If you are lucky enough to know a gem of a fish dealer who has fresh fish and who keeps it properly displayed on beds of ice, then you can ask his advice about the amount of fish you should buy. But if you're on your own, then a good rule of thumb is to get a pound of fish per person when you are buying the whole fish with bones and head intact, and ⅓ to ½ pound per person if you are buying fillets.

Storage: When you get the fish home, rewrap it in plastic or place it in a covered dish and put it in the coldest part of the refrigerator. Some people like to pack the dish full of ice, creating a miniature fish-market case, but this is not necessary. Just be sure to cook it within 24 hours. If you get a last-minute invitation to dinner, wrap the mackerel or halibut tightly in aluminum foil and pop it in the freezer, or else cook it and plan to serve it the next day as a fish salad. Just don't let it sit uncooked in your refrigerator for more than 24 hours. Before cooking, wash it and pat it dry.

The exceptions to this rule are the fish that are bought already in a state of preservation: frozen, smoked or canned. Because of the unreliability of transporters, frozen fish can be either a close second to fresh fish or a miserable disaster. Sometimes it is simply all that you can get. If you store it in the coldest part of your freezer and use it as soon as possible, it will probably be acceptable. Thin fillets don't have to be thawed before they are cooked. However, if you have a whole frozen fish, then you

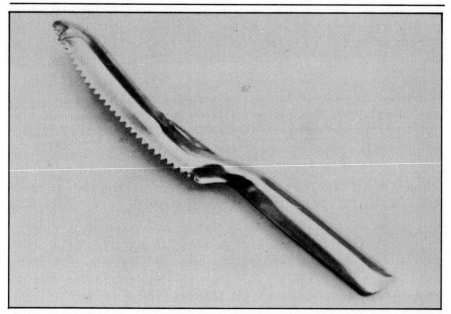

Stainless-Steel Fish Scaler. The business end of this solid fish scaler is curved upward so that it won't break the skin of the fish; the other end is rolled into an easily-grasped handle. The scaler's open design makes it easy to clean.

should defrost it in the refrigerator or under cold running water before you cook it. Fish that is left to defrost slowly on a kitchen counter loses its firmness.

As for smoked fish, it is rather perishable, although not so much as it was in its pre-smoked condition. Smoking is, in fact, a kind of half-cooking. If you intend to keep smoked fish beyond a week, however, you should wrap it tightly in foil and freeze it: large pieces freeze better than thin slices. Canned fish, on the other hand, keeps for many months and is usually one of the staple foods on the pantry shelf. In the opinion of many cooks, cans of tuna, salmon, mackerel, sardines, herring fillets, gefilte fish, shrimp, crabmeat and minced clams are an essential part of any well-stocked kitchen. They can't equal the fresh, but prove to be more reliable than the frozen.

Cleaning Fish: Even if a cook never goes near a mountain stream or an oyster bed, he or she should be able to perform certain basic procedures of cleaning and scaling fish and opening mollusks. After all, every one has friends who fish, and who can be counted on to share the catch! With the right equipment, this is not difficult.

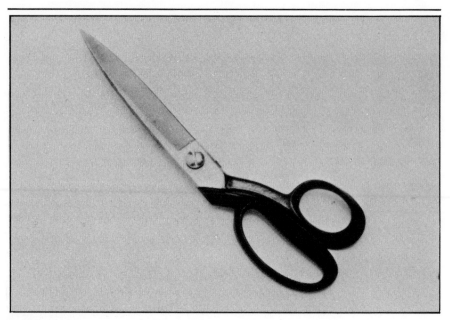

Fish Shears. Serious scissors are a boon to fish cookery: a practical device for cutting through the belly of the fish, snipping around the gills, trimming off fins, or removing heads and tails.

To scale a fish, place it on a counter, holding it firmly by the tail with one hand and, with a good scaler in the other hand, scrape towards the head, removing the scales as you do so. This works best on wet fish, so soak the fish in cold water for a few minutes before you begin, and rinse it frequently as you work.

If you have the stomach for it, you can then clean the fish by slitting the whole length of the belly from the anal opening to the head. Pull out the intestines. (This step is essential for fishermen to learn, since enzymes in the fish's gastrointestinal system will cause it to deteriorate rapidly if it is left ungutted. Bluefish, bass and weakfish must be gutted immediately.) Cut around the fins near the head and pull them off. If you like, remove the head, the dorsal or back fin, and the tail with a good pair of shears, and rinse the fish well in cold running water.

Filleting and Skinning: Filleting and skinning are a little more difficult to master, but they can be done at home by anyone who has a little patience and a sharp, flexible knife. A filleting knife is especially helpful. Fillets are made by laying the fish flat and cutting through the flesh to the backbone, just behind the head. Then, holding the knife blade parallel to the back-

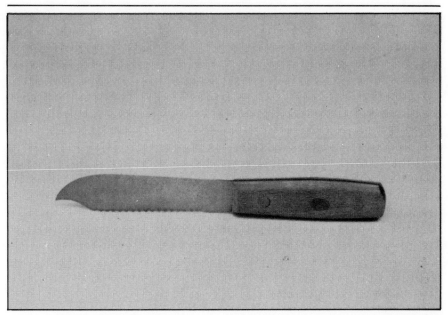

All-Purpose Fish Knife. If you feel that one fish knife is all you need, this sturdy little instrument would be a good choice. The serrated back edge is designed for scaling, and the cutting edge will slice small steaks.

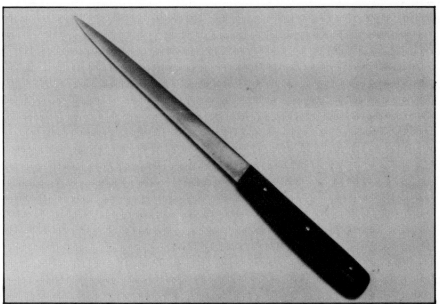

Flexible Filleting Knife. From France comes an extremely sharp, flexible knife with a thin blade that's useful for boning jobs as well as for filleting small fish.

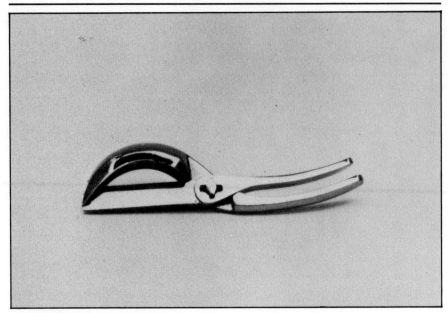

Steel Clam Opener. With more leverage than offered by a knife, this scissor-like tool will separate the shell of a clam placed vertically between its jaws. The forked tip of the stainless-steel blade can be used to remove the clam from its shell, and the implement comes apart for easy cleaning.

bone, tease the flesh away from the ribs, first on one side and then on the other, cutting from the head toward the tail. Skinning is done by placing a fillet flat on your working surface (work on layers of old newspapers for easy clean-up) with the skin side down. Insert the knife blade between the flesh and the skin at the tail end and, holding tightly onto the tail, work the skin free along the whole length of the fish.

Cleaning Mollusks: Many people clean mollusks by soaking them for a few hours in cold water until they give up their sand and impurities, then they scrub the shells. Others simply omit the soaking and scrub the shells with a tough wire brush or scouring pad. It's usually best to do both. When opening shellfish, you should have a top-notch clam opener, a combination church-key and knife. Insert the edge of the opener into the hinge of the shell, turning it to pry and lift the upper shell. When it is lifted, you can cut the hinge muscle with the blade. Always do this over a bowl, so that you catch all the juices that spill out, and save them to use in sauces and steaming liquids.

You can get more complete directions on cleaning from a book on

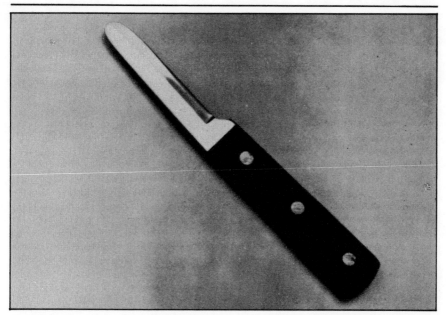

Stainless-Steel Clam Knife. The clam is a more tractable creature than the oyster, with a more clearly revealed opening between its shells. Hence, clam knives have blunt rather than sharp tips, which minimizes the danger of cutting into the meat.

game fishing or by cosying up to your local fish dealer. We urge you, however, to buy a good filleting knife, heavy shears, an oyster knife, and a scaler before you attempt to do any seafood-butchery on your own.

Cooking Seafood: Most cook books will offer you a number of seafood recipes, all depending on a limited range of techniques that are easily mastered. After you can perform these basic procedures, it's all a matter of varying the seasonings and the sauces; adding parsley and almonds here or white grapes there, stewing in tomato sauce or in fish stock, broiling with fennel or over charcoal. None of the techniques is difficult to master. The trick, finally, is to have fresh fish and to know when it is properly cooked. Undercooked fish is not to American tastes; overcooked fish falls apart and loses its character. Fish is cooked when its internal temperature reaches 140 degrees; its tissues break down after 145 degrees. But unless you plan to use a tiny instant thermometer, this would be a good time to repeat the Canadian Fisheries rule about timing. Remember that this guide applies whether you're baking a whole fish in foil or throwing a fillet into a pan of melted butter. It works over blazing charcoal or over barely-

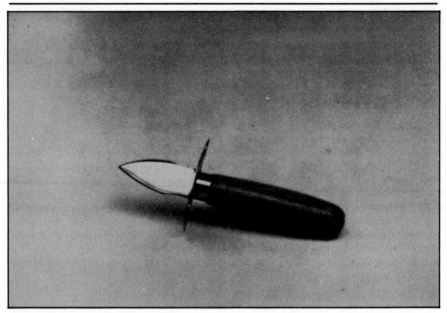

Stainless-Steel Oyster Knife. A hefty, comfortable handle on this oyster knife gives you good purchase as you force open the shells of an understandably reluctant oyster. A large, cutlass-like bolster protects the hand and provides some leverage for the blade.

simmering court bouillon. (This rule does not apply for shellfish. Heavy shells and irregular shapes call for individual treatment.) *Cook fresh fish for ten minutes for every inch of thickness measured at its widest part, and double the time per inch for frozen fish.*

In the absence of a Canadian Fisheries rule for shellfish, try to remember to cook it at the lowest heat possible, and for the shortest cooking period possible. Remember that cooking serves to make shellfish tougher, not more tender, and that over-cooking will also toughen it.

Attending to this rule, you can cook fish in any of five basic ways. Fish can be baked: that is, cooked uncovered in the surrounding heat of an oven. It can be broiled, either in the range or over charcoal. It can be fried: cooked in deep fat or in a little butter, with or without breading or a batter coating. It can be steamed over liquid. And it can be poached in water, court bouillon or wine, or in a soup or chowder. If home cooks can master these five basic techniques, then they are well on the way to being first-rate fish cooks.

Baking: Baked fish is often left whole, its head and backbone adding

Fillet of Sole Dish. A dish for fillet of sole should be deep enough to hold liquid for oven poaching, but low enough to go under the broiler for browning. In addition, an unglazed base will better absorb oven heat.

flavor to the meat. Frequently it is stuffed and sewed together and put in a pan which is strewn with chopped vegetables, then cooked in a 450-degree oven. For how long? Refer to the Canadian rule, already mentioned, but be sure to measure the fish *after,* not before, it is stuffed.

Broiling: Broiled fish is the darling of dieters, since it is so low in calories. If it is to be grilled over charcoal, you must have a long-handled wire rack, either a flat one for grilling fillets and split fish, or a fat fish-shaped one for grilling whole fish. Otherwise, there is simply no way that you can oil the skin well enough to keep it from sticking to the broiler rack. Lobsters and crabs do well on a charcoal grill: split, cleaned and repeatedly painted with seasoned melted butter.

Frying: Fried fish is both the most plebeian and the most aristocratic form of fish cookery. On the one hand we have fish-and-chips and fish-stick sandwiches, hot crunchy morsels of anonymous white fish which, served with tartar sauce and fried potatoes, are satisfying snacks. On the upper end of the scale there are fillets *sautés meunière,* given a brief time in a

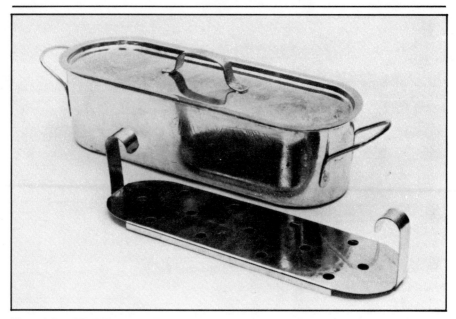

Tinned-Steel Fish Poacher. Fish poachers come in a range of sizes—from about 10″ to 36″ long. French poachers, like this one, have double-handled tinned-steel racks to hold the fish in, and then lift it out of, simmering liquid.

pan of bubbling butter to crisp the lightly-floured or crumbed surface, and then arranged on a plate and dressed with butter, a squeeze of lemon juice and parsley. Fried fish of both varieties requires careful attention to the temperature of the fat, which should be heated to 365 degrees before the fish is put in, and then brought rapidly back up to that heat. All shellfish and mollusks are wonderful when they are battered or breaded and then deep-fried.

Steaming and Boiling: Steamed fish is usually identified with the cuisines of China and Japan. For steaming, it's very convenient to have special equipment to hold the fish above the simmering liquid. Bass and other fish cooked by steaming retain a natural sweetness. When fish is actually cooked in liquid, it should be poached—not boiled. The water should barely simmer to keep the fish from breaking apart. Shellfish, however, tolerate rougher treatment. For example, lobsters are always bought alive and should never be killed until you cook them. If boiled lobster is the dish, you will have to plunge the still-active lobster into boiling water. If it's any consolation, ichthyologists tell us that lobsters have very primitive nervous

Copper Fish Poacher. Lined with stainless steel, this attractive fish poacher also has a versatile stainless-steel rack. The handles of the rack can be used upright, as shown, for poaching, or they can be turned under the rack to support it, if you would rather steam the fish.

systems and don't feel any pain during this procedure. Crabs can be steamed, poached or boiled, like lobsters, except that they are usually treated with more seasonings in the process since the flavorings can penetrate their thinner shells.

Finally, there are soups, stews and chowders. Chowder is one of the great American dishes, usually made on a base of milk, onions and salt pork—ask any New Englander—while other soups may have any sort of base at all, from the saffron-enriched court bouillon of *bouillabaisse* to the thyme-sparked tomato sauce of *cioppino*.

As you see, there's nothing very difficult about cooking fish and shellfish. Since they are so good when they are given the lightest cooking possible, we should not hesitate to be more adventurous with them. Try grilling salmon over charcoal, slipping cut-up scallops into a pasta sauce, turning conch into a *seviche* by marinating it in lime juice. Fish on Friday is a thing of the past; no reason now to limit it to that one day of the week. Once you have begun to cook fish and shellfish, it will become a regular part of your diet.

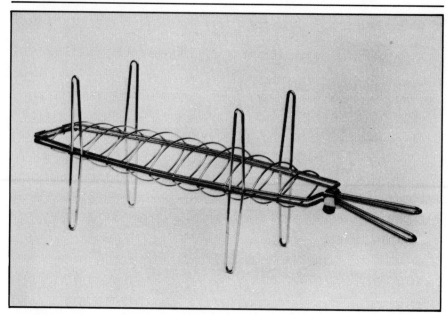

Fish Grill. A classic tinned-steel, fish-shaped grill is equipped with legs that allow it to stand above glowing coals. When one side of the fish is done, flip the grill to finish the other side. The grill may be used outside or in the fireplace.

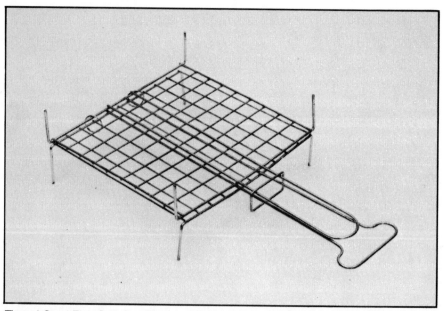

Tinned-Steel Fish Grill. For fillets, a grill should have legs on top and bottom so it can stand on its own to cook both sides of the fish. Another feature to look for is close spacing of the wires to prevent the flesh of small fish from slipping into the fire.

Basic Cooking Equipment: There are certain things which you should have in your kitchen to help you in becoming a good fish cook. We've mentioned a fish scaler, a flexible filleting knife, a clam opener, an oyster knife and a strong pair of kitchen shears. For scrubbing the outsides of shells, you'll also need one of those tough little pads made of coiled copper or steel. Cooking the fish requires even fewer pieces of special equipment. You ought to have a poacher-steamer, a good heavy skillet, a baking dish and a rack for grilling, either a flat rack for holding fillets or a big fish-shaped one that can stand on its own wire legs in the bed of coals of the grill or even in your fireplace. You might want an instant thermometer to tell you when the lobster is done. And in honor of the Canadian Fisheries and Marine Service, keep a ruler handy.

You are now on the road to fish cookery. Whether you are planning to grill a simple skewer-full of sea scallops or create a complicated lobster Bellevue, a piece of grilled halibut or a rich bowl of fish chowder, these basic techniques, plus a respect for the fragile texture of the fish, are all that you will need in order to succeed. There was a time when fish was cheap. Now, because of labor costs, international over-fishing, and the new attention to seafood as a source of low-fat protein, prices have risen so that they equal or surpass the cost of beef. It's never pleasant to pay more money for food, but it is fitting, nevertheless, that fish should cost as much as meat does. It is a food that should be chosen with care, preserved with attention and cooked with respect. And above all, enjoyed.

Fish

BAKED BASS WITH STUFFED FRUIT

Paula Wolfert

6 servings

4 POUNDS CLEANED, SCALED, GUTTED AND SPLIT SEA OR STRIPED BASS
1 TABLESPOON SALT
FRESHLY GROUND PEPPER
2½ TABLESPOONS GRANULATED RICE ("CREAM OF RICE")
½ CUP WHOLE, BLANCHED ALMONDS (ABOUT 5 OUNCES)
¾ TEASPOON GROUND GINGER
2 TO 3 TEASPOONS SUGAR
6 TABLESPOONS BUTTER
1 POUND PITTED DATES OR PRUNES (2 CUPS)
2 TABLESPOONS CHOPPED ONION
½ TO 1 TEASPOON GROUND CINNAMON

1. Wash the fish rapidly under running water. Pat it dry with paper towels, then rub it with salt and pepper.

2. Bring ¾-cup of water to a boil in a small saucepan. Sprinkle with ½ teaspoon salt and quickly pour in the granulated rice. Boil for 30 seconds, beating well. Turn off the heat and allow it to stand, covered, a few minutes, then cool.

3. Grind the almonds and mix them with the cooled rice mixture, reserving 2 tablespoons of ground almonds for later use. Add ½ teaspoon of the ground ginger, 2 to 3 teaspoons sugar, ¼ teaspoon freshly ground black pepper and 1 tablespoon of the butter to the almond-rice mixture. Blend well.

4. Open the dates or prunes and stuff each with about ½ teaspoon of the almond-rice mixture. If the dates are small, push two together to form a "sandwich."

5. Sew the opening of the fish three-quarters of the way, filling the stomach cavity with as many stuffed fruits as possible. Complete sewing.

6. Preheat the oven to 350 F. Butter an ovenproof dish and place the stuffed fish on its side. Pour ½ cup water over it and sprinkle with salt and pepper and the remaining ¼ teaspoon of ginger. Add the chopped onion and remaining stuffed fruit and dot the fish with the remaining 5 tablespoons of butter.

7. Bake 45 minutes on the middle shelf of the oven, basting frequently.

8. Remove the fish from the oven, then raise the oven heat to its highest setting. Untie the thread, pull out the stuffed fruit from the fish's cavity and place it around the fish. Sprinkle both fish and fruit with ½ to 1 teaspoon ground

---

cinnamon and the remaining 2 tablespoons of ground almonds. Set the baking dish on the highest rack of the oven and bake the fish until golden brown and crusty (about 15 minutes). Serve at once.

NORTHERN WISCONSIN FISH BOIL

Ruth Ellen Church

For 20 hungry people

40 LAKE TROUT STEAKS, 1½
INCHES THICK (OR SUBSTITUTE
ANY SIZABLE, NOT TOO BONY,
FIRM-FLESHED SMALL WHOLE
FISH OR STEAKS OF HALIBUT,
HAKE, COD, OR SALMON)
20 OR MORE MEDIUM-SIZED
POTATOES
20 OR MORE WHOLE MEDIUM-
SIZED ONIONS (OPTIONAL)*
40 EARS CORN (OPTIONAL)*

You need a huge kettle that will hold everything, if possible. The corn may be cooked separately, if necessary. You also will need wire baskets or nets to keep the ingredients separate for cooking.

1. Fill a large kettle at least half-way with water and bring it to a boil over a well-made outdoor fire. Then add ½ pound salt for each 2 gallons of water.

2. Scrub the potatoes, leaving the skin on, and cut a little piece from each end, for flavor penetration. Skin the onions and remove all but the innermost husks from the corn, or husk it completely, if you prefer.

3. Lower the potatoes and onions in one or two nets or baskets into the boiling water.

4. After 15 minutes, add the corn.

5. Test the potatoes after 18 to 20 minutes. They should be almost cooked before the fish goes into the pot, in its own basket or net, preferably the former. Keep the pot boiling and test the fish after 8 minutes or so. When the flesh flakes, it is done.

6. Next is the "overboil," which is spectacular in the North Woods. It is a means of removing the fish oils, it is said. Otherwise you should do some skimming as the pot boils. For the overboil, kerosene is thrown on the fire at the base of the pot. The flames leap (be careful!) and the salty water boils over, putting out the fire. Now you call your guests. Pitchers of melted butter, bowls of cole slaw, rye bread, and cherry and blueberry pies should be on hand. This is a typical northern Wisconsin fish boil and it is fun for all.

   * The onions and corn are not so typical. Most boils feature potatoes and fish alone, but with a big enough kettle the extras are easy.

FISH LOAF WITH MALTAISE SAUCE
(ORANGE-FLAVORED HOLLANDAISE)

Jeanne Lesem

4 to 6 servings

1½ POUNDS FISH FILLETS, ANY MILD-FLAVORED FRESH OR SALT-WATER VARIETY SUCH AS CATFISH, PIKE, COD, HADDOCK, POLLOCK, SEA TROUT (ALSO CALLED WEAKFISH) OR WHITING
1 SMALL ONION
1 MEDIUM-SIZED CARROT
1 TEASPOON FRESHLY GRATED ORANGE PEEL
⅓ CUP ORANGE JUICE, FRESH OR RECONSTITUTED FROZEN

2 TABLESPOONS MATZO MEAL OR UNSALTED CRACKER CRUMBS
½ TEASPOON SALT
¼ TEASPOON FRESHLY GROUND PEPPER
¼ TEASPOON SUGAR
1 LARGE EGG
3 TABLESPOONS BUTTER, MELTED AND COOLED
WATERCRESS OR PARSLEY FOR GARNISH

1. Put the fish fillets through a grinder, using a medium blade, or chop them to medium texture in a food processor.

2. Peel and grind the onion and carrot.

3. Grate the orange peel and prepare the orange juice, reserving excess peel and juice, if any, for other uses.

4. In a bowl of at least 1-quart capacity, mix all the ingredients, except for the garnish, until evenly blended.

5. Scrape the mixture into a well-buttered or oiled 1-quart mold or ovenproof baking dish.

6. Place on the center shelf of a preheated 375 F. oven and bake 1 hour, until firm.

7. Remove from the oven and let stand 10 to 15 minutes to re-absorb the juices.

Maltaise Sauce:
1 LARGE EGG YOLK
¼ TEASPOON SALT (IF USING UNSALTED BUTTER)
¼ TEASPOON PAPRIKA
2 TO 3 PINCHES CAYENNE
1 TO 2 TEASPOONS ORANGE JUICE
¼ TO ½ TEASPOON FRESHLY GRATED ORANGE PEEL
1 CUP MELTED BUTTER, WARM

1. To make the Maltaise sauce, rinse a small, deep bowl (not aluminum—it would discolor the sauce) with very hot, but not boiling, water. Dry well.

2. Place the egg yolk, salt, paprika, cayenne, 1 teaspoon of the orange juice and the grated orange peel in the bowl. Beat until the mixture is well blended and pale yellow. Then begin dribbling in melted butter in a thin stream. When the mixture thickens perceptibly, add the remaining butter somewhat faster. If the mixture becomes too thick before all the butter is added, add the extra spoonful of juice or an equal amount of boiling water.

3. Serve at once or set the bowl in a shallow pan of hot, but not boiling, water and drop a few slivers of butter on the surface to melt and prevent a skin from forming. The melted butter can be stirred into the sauce just before serving.

4. To serve, unmold the fish loaf on a serving plate and garnish it with watercress or parsley sprigs or serve it directly from the casserole. Pass the sauce separately. (Leftovers are delicious served with slightly warmed, leftover Maltaise sauce, dill mayonnaise, or sour cream mixed with drained red horseradish sauce.)

SALMON MOUSSE

Michael Batterberry

10 first course servings/24 cocktail spread servings

2 TABLESPOONS PLAIN GELATIN (2 PACKETS)
⅔ CUP BOTTLED CLAM JUICE
2 7¾-OUNCE CANS SOCKEYE RED SALMON
1½ TABLESPOONS ANCHOVY PASTE
2 TABLESPOONS CAPERS
2 WHOLE SCALLIONS, CUT IN ½-INCH LENGTHS
¼ CUP LEMON JUICE

1 TABLESPOON DRIED DILL WEED
8 DROPS TABASCO OR HOT SAUCE
1 PINT CHILLED HEAVY WHIPPING CREAM
½ PINT SOUR CREAM
PINCH SALT
LEMON JUICE
FRESH DILL OR COARSELY CHOPPED WATERCRESS LEAVES
CAPERS FOR GARNISH

1. Sprinkle the gelatin over the cold clam juice in an enameled saucepan. When softened, stir the gelatin over very low heat until it is completely dissolved and set it aside to cool at room temperature.

2. If using a blender, the following should be done in 2 or 3 batches; with a food processor, it can be done all at once. Grind to a purée the salmon, anchovy paste, capers, scallions, lemon juice, dill weed, Tabasco or hot sauce and gelatin-clam syrup. If using a blender you may have to add a bit more clam juice to keep the blades in motion—however, use as little as possible.

3. Whip the heavy cream in a chilled bowl with chilled beaters or whisk until stiff.

4. Fold the salmon purée into the whipped cream until the mixture is even in color.

5. As this recipe makes about 8 cups, choose an appropriately sized mold, preferably loaf-shaped. Coat it well with salad oil and fill it with the mousse. Refrigerate for at least 6 to 8 hours (or overnight).

6. Unmold and "ice" the mousse with sour cream beaten smooth with a large pinch of salt and a squeeze of lemon. Decorate with fresh dill or chopped watercress leaves and a palm full of capers.

STRIPED BASS WITH AROMATIC SEASONINGS (PSARI PLAKI)

Vilma Liacouras Chantiles

4 servings

4 STRIPED SEA BASS STEAKS
WEIGHING ABOUT ½ POUND
EACH (OR OTHER NON-OILY FISH
STEAKS), WASHED AND DRIED
SALT
FRESHLY GROUND PEPPER
JUICE OF 1 LEMON
⅓ CUP FINE OLIVE OIL
1 ONION OR 2 SHALLOTS, MINCED
2 CLOVES GARLIC, CRUSHED
½ CUP DRY WHITE WINE

3 FRESH OR CANNED PLUM
TOMATOES, CHOPPED, WITH
SOME JUICE
SMALL BUNCH FRESH DILL,
CHOPPED OR SUBSTITUTE 1
TABLESPOON DRIED DILL
3 TABLESPOONS CHOPPED
PARSLEY
½ CUP FRESH SPINACH LEAVES,
CHOPPED
4 LEMON SLICES FOR GARNISH

1. Arrange the fish steaks in a casserole. Dust them lightly with salt and pepper, and sprinkle with lemon juice. Marinate them while preparing sauce.

2. Preheat the oven to 350 F.

3. In a medium-sized pan, heat 2 tablespoons of the olive oil and sauté the onion for 1 minute, stirring constantly. Add the garlic, wine and tomatoes with some juice. Simmer for 15 minutes.

4. Stir in the dill, all but a tablespoon of the parsley, the spinach and the remaining olive oil during the last 5 minutes of cooking. There should be enough sauce to cover the fish. If not, add more wine and tomato juice.

5. Spoon the sauce over the fish. Bake in a moderate oven for 20 minutes or until fork tender.

6. Remove the fish to a warm platter and keep warm. If the sauce is thin, pour it into a small pan and boil it down to ½ cup. Pour it over the fish.

7. Sprinkle the fish with the remaining parsley and with lemon juice.

8. Serve with Greek salad, crusty bread and retsina wine.

SHAD ROE MOUSSE WITH SORREL SAUCE

Helen McCully

6 servings

3 PAIRS SMALL SHAD ROE
3 CUPS HEAVY CREAM
3 EGG WHITES
SALT
FRESHLY GROUND PEPPER
PAPRIKA

1. Butter a 9-inch ring mold (not aluminum) very thoroughly and refrigerate.

2. Cut the pairs of shad roe apart and remove as much of the filmy skin as possible. Purée, about half at a time, in an electric food processor with a steel blade. Place the purée in a generous bowl with the cream, egg whites and seasonings to taste. Beat steadily with an electric beater for about 10 minutes.

3. Pour the mixture into the prepared mold and place in the refrigerator for 30 minutes or so.

4. To bake, place the mold in a baking pan, pour in enough boiling water to reach two-thirds up the side of the mold. Bake in a preheated 350 F. oven on the middle rack for 1 hour and 15 minutes, or until a knife inserted in the center comes out clean.
   While the mousse is baking, make the sorrel sauce, beginning with a *béchamel* sauce.

White Sauce (*béchamel*):
2 TABLESPOONS BUTTER
1½ TABLESPOONS FLOUR
1½ CUPS MILK
SALT
WHITE PEPPER

1. Melt the butter in a heavy saucepan (not aluminum) over low heat. Stir in 1½ tablespoons flour and cook slowly, stirring constantly, until the butter and flour froth—about 3 minutes—without browning (this is the white *roux,* or *roux blanc*). Remove from the heat.

2. Add 1½ cups milk, and beat vigorously with a wire whip to incorporate the *roux* thoroughly. Place the pan over moderately high heat and cook, stirring with a whip, until the *béchamel* comes to a boil. Boil for 1 minute, stirring constantly. Remove from the heat and beat in salt and white pepper.

Sorrel Sauce:
1½ CUPS MEDIUM WHITE SAUCE
   (*BÉCHAMEL*)
½ CUP HEAVY CREAM
SALT
WHITE PEPPER
½ TABLESPOON BUTTER
¼ CUP (APPROXIMATELY) FRESH
   SORREL, CUT IN FINE MATCH-
   STICK STRIPS
2 TABLESPOONS CAPERS, WELL
   DRAINED

1. Bring the white sauce to a simmer, then beat in the cream, a small amount at a time, until the sauce is lightly thickened. Season to taste with salt and white pepper. Set aside for the moment.

2. Melt the butter. When foaming, add the shredded sorrel and simmer for 5 to 6 minutes. Strain off any surplus juice and stir the sorrel into the cream sauce. Bring to a simmer again, then add the capers.

3. To serve, unmold the mousse onto a warm serving platter. Spoon some of the sorrel sauce over the ring and serve the remainder on the side.

HOT FISH CANAPÉS

Jane Moulton

56 bite-sized morsels

¾ CUP MAYONNAISE (NOT SALAD
  DRESSING)
½ CUP FINELY CUT CELERY
⅓ CUP CHOPPED SCALLIONS
3 TABLESPOONS CHOPPED
  PIMIENTO-STUFFED OLIVES OR
  SALAD OLIVES
1 CUP GRATED SHARP CHEDDAR
  CHEESE

1 TABLESPOON DRY OR 3
  TABLESPOONS CHOPPED FRESH
  PARSLEY
2 CUPS (FROM 1 POUND) COOKED
  FISH FILLETS IN BITE-SIZED
  PIECES
28 SLICES BUTTERED BREAD WITH
  CRUSTS REMOVED

1. In a mixing bowl, combine the mayonnaise, celery, scallions, olives, cheese and parsley. Fold in the cooked fish.

2. Spread half the unbuttered sides of bread with the fish mixture. Top with the remaining slices, butter side up.

3. Grill until golden brown. Cut into quarters and serve as appetizers.

SMOKED HADDOCK ASPIC

Maurice Moore-Betty

6 servings

1½ CUPS CHICKEN, VEAL OR FISH
  STOCK
1 SMALL ONION, THINLY SLICED
1 EGGSHELL, CRUSHED
1 EGG WHITE, LIGHTLY BEATEN
1 ENVELOPE (1 TABLESPOON)
  UNFLAVORED GELATIN
8 OUNCES SMOKED HADDOCK
EQUAL AMOUNTS OF MILK AND
  WATER TO COVER FISH

¼ CUP RESERVED POACHING
  LIQUID
GRATED RIND OF 1 LEMON
¾ CUP HEAVY CREAM
WHITE SEEDLESS GRAPES
SALT
PEPPER
NUTMEG
WATERCRESS FOR GARNISH

1. In a saucepan, combine the stock, onion, crushed eggshell and egg white.

2. Simmer for 10 minutes, then cool for 20 minutes.

3. Strain the mixture through 3 or 4 thicknesses of cheesecloth to clarify it.

4. Soften the gelatin by sprinkling it over ½ cup of the strained stock. Dissolve it over very low heat and then add it to the clarified stock. Cool before using.

5. Cover the fish with the milk-water mixture and bring it slowly to a boil (the mixture boils over easily and makes an incredible mess if not watched). Reduce to a simmer and cook for a minute or two. Drain the fish, reserving ¼ cup of the poaching liquid, and then flake the meat with a fork.

6. Purée the flaked fish and the ¼ cup reserved poaching liquid in a food processor. Scrape the purée into a clean bowl and stir in ¼ cup liquid aspic and the lemon rind.

7. Whip the heavy cream until stiff and incorporate it into the fish mixture. Season to taste with salt, pepper and nutmeg. Chill.

8. Into six ½-cup molds, spoon 1 tablespoon aspic and allow it to set in the refrigerator.

9. Take the molds from the refrigerator. Arrange enough grapes on the aspic in each mold to cover it completely. Add 2 tablespoons of aspic to cover the grapes and return the molds to the refrigerator to set.

10. Fill the molds with fish purée and chill for at least 2 hours before unmolding.

11. To unmold, wring out a clean kitchen towel in hot water and wrap it around each mold. Turn the aspic out on a serving dish and garnish it with watercress.

BROILED CURRIED FISH FILLETS

Emanuel and Madeline Greenberg

2 to 3 servings

¼ CUP SOFT BREAD CRUMBS
¼ CUP GRATED PARMESAN, OR
   OTHER SHARP CHEESE
½ TEASPOON PAPRIKA
¼ TEASPOON CURRY POWDER
SALT TO TASTE
PEPPER TO TASTE
1 POUND FRESH FILLETS, ABOUT
   ½-INCH THICK
SALAD OIL
4 TABLESPOONS MELTED BUTTER
   OR OLIVE OIL
LEMON WEDGES OR TARRAGON
   VINEGAR

1. Preheat broiler to 550 F. Heat the broiling pan.

2. Combine the bread crumbs, cheese and seasonings. Dredge the top of the fish with the crumb mixture.

3. Brush the heated pan generously with salad oil and place the fillets in it. Drizzle with 2 tablespoons of the melted butter or oil.

4. Broil 3 inches from the heat for 3 minutes. Baste with the remaining butter or oil and broil 3 minutes more.

5. Lift the fillets from the pan with 2 spatulas and place them on a warm serving platter.

6. Serve with lemon wedges or sprinkle lightly with tarragon vinegar.

STRIPED BASS BROILED WITH VINEGAR

Carole Lalli

4 servings

1 3-POUND STRIPED BASS,
   FILLETED
OLIVE OIL
SALT
PEPPER
½ TEASPOON DRIED OREGANO
4 OR 5 LARGE GARLIC CLOVES, IN
   THICK SLICES
½ CUP RED WINE VINEGAR
   (APPROXIMATELY)
2 TABLESPOONS CHOPPED ITALIAN
   OR CURLY PARSLEY

1. Brush the fish with olive oil, sprinkle it with salt, pepper and oregano and broil it under medium heat in a preheated broiler for 5 minutes.

2. Toss the garlic cloves over the fillets; pour the vinegar over them, raising the heat to high and broil for five minutes more. Sprinkle generously with chopped Italian parsley before serving.

LAOTIAN FISH SOUP (KAENG SOM PLA)

Raymond Sokolov with thanks to Alan Davidson

4 servings

1 POUND FRESHWATER FISH
2 OR 3 STALKS FRESH, OR 1
   TABLESPOON DRIED, LEMON
   GRASS (KNOWN AS *SEREK* OR
   TAKRAI IN ORIENTAL MARKETS)
   (SEE NOTE BELOW)
½ TEASPOON SALT
½ TEASPOON MONOSODIUM
   GLUTAMATE (OPTIONAL)
2 TABLESPOONS *NAM PLA*
   (BOTTLED THAI OR OTHER
SOUTHEAST ASIAN FISH SAUCE
   SUCH AS *NUOC NAM* FROM
   VIETNAM)
1 LARGE TOMATO, QUARTERED
3 SCALLIONS, TRIMMED AND
   SLICED IN THIN ROUNDS
2 TABLESPOONS CHOPPED
   CORIANDER *CILANTRO* OR
   CHINESE PARSLEY)
JUICE OF ½ LIME

1. Clean, scale and wash the fish. Then cut it into crosswise sections about 1-inch thick.

2. Crush the lemon grass stalks (or simply measure out the dried lemon grass) and combine it with salt, MSG (if used) and 3 cups of water in a 3-to-4-quart saucepan. Bring to a boil, reduce the heat and simmer for 10 minutes.

3. Add the fish sections and *nam pla* to the lemon grass broth. Return to a boil, add the tomato quarters, reduce the heat and simmer gently for 10 to 15 minutes, uncovered.

4. Remove soup from the heat. Discard lemon grass stalks, if any. Garnish the soup with scallion rounds and chopped coriander. Put a few drops of lime juice in each soup bowl. Pour in the soup, taking care that each bowl receives its fair share of fish and other solid ingredients.

Note: Exotic ingredients are available at Thailand Food Corp., 2445 Broadway, New York, New York or by mail from H. Roth and Son, 1577 First Avenue, New York, New York 10028.

BRAISED SOY FISH

Gloria Bley Miller

4 servings

4 DRIED BLACK CHINESE MUSHROOMS
2 TO 3 SCALLIONS
6 WATER CHESTNUTS
1 CLOVE GARLIC
½ CUP CHICKEN STOCK
2 TABLESPOONS SOY SAUCE
1 TABLESPOON MEDIUM-DRY SHERRY

½ TEASPOON SUGAR
1 TEASPOON SALT
1½ TO 2 POUNDS WHOLE FISH (SEA BASS OR RED SNAPPER)
FLOUR
4 TO 6 TABLESPOONS PEANUT OIL

1. Soak the mushrooms for 30 minutes in hot water to soften.

2. Squeeze excess water from the mushrooms and reserve the mushrooms and soaking water. Cut off and discard the stems, then cut the mushrooms into strips. Cut the scallions into ½-inch lengths. Slice the water chestnuts. Crush the garlic lightly with the side of a knife blade so that it splits but remains intact, then peel.

3. In a small bowl, combine half a cup of the mushroom soaking water, the chicken stock, soy sauce, sherry, sugar and ½ teaspoon of the salt.

4. Rinse the fish in cold water. Dry it well inside and out. Score the fish on both sides by making three parallel slashes about 1½ inches apart, each about 1-inch deep.

5. Sprinkle the fish with the remaining ½ teaspoon of salt, then lightly with flour, rubbing it gently over the surface to coat it.

6. In a pan or skillet large enough for the fish, heat the oil. Add the garlic clove. Let it brown lightly and discard it. Add the fish and fry it until golden on each side.

7. Add the seasoned stock mixture, mushrooms and scallions. Bring to a boil. Reduce the heat to medium. Cover the pan and cook for 15 minutes.

8. Gently turn the fish over, taking care not to break the skin. Cook covered for another 15 minutes.

9. Transfer the fish to a large heated platter. Pour the sauce over it and serve.

PARMESAN FISH FILLETS

Jane Moulton

6 to 8 servings

2 CUPS FRESH BREAD CRUMBS
  (FROM 4 SLICES BREAD)
1 CUP SOUR CREAM
⅔ CUP GRATED PARMESAN
  CHEESE
1¼ TEASPOONS GARLIC SALT
3 POUNDS FRESH COD, SOLE OR
  OTHER FILLETS

1. In a mixing bowl or food processor, combine all the ingredients except the fish.

2. Wash the fish, dry it with toweling and place it skin side down in a 13-by-9-inch (or equivalent) baking dish.

3. Spread the bread crumb-cheese paste over the fish.

4. Bake in a preheated 450 F. oven for 15 or 20 minutes—just until the fish begins to flake when pulled with a fork. The fish should be nicely browned, but if it isn't, place it under the broiler just before it's done. Don't overcook it.

CHINESE FISH FILLETS WITH WALNUTS

Gloria Bley Miller

4 servings

2 LARGE FLOUNDER FILLETS
2 THIN SLICES SMOKED HAM
2 SCALLIONS
2 SMALL SLICES FRESH GINGER
  ROOT
1 EGG
1 TABLESPOON MEDIUM-DRY
  SHERRY
1 TEASPOON CORNSTARCH
1 TEASPOON SOY SAUCE
½ TEASPOON SUGAR
½ TEASPOON SALT
½ CUP WALNUT MEATS
OIL FOR DEEP-FRYING

1. Cut the flounder fillets in half lengthwise, then in half crosswise. Cut the ham into roughly the same dimensions, but slightly smaller. Mince the scallions and ginger root.

2. Beat the egg in a bowl. Blend in the sherry, cornstarch, soy sauce, sugar and salt, along with the minced scallions and ginger root.

3. Chop the walnuts fine. Spread them out on a flat surface.

4. Heat the oil to 350 F. Dip the fish pieces into the egg mixture to coat them, then coat one side only with walnuts.

5. Wrap each piece (walnut-side out) around a piece of ham and roll up. Fasten it securely with a toothpick or tie it with thread or string.

6. Gradually add the fish rolls to the oil so they don't clump together. Deep-fry until golden (about 3 minutes). Drain on paper toweling and remove the fastening. Serve at once.

POMPANO EN PAPILLOTE (POMPANO IN A PAPER BAG)

Nathalie Dupree

4 servings

4 POMPANO, ¾ TO 1 POUND EACH, CLEANED AND SCALED
FRESHLY DRIED FENNEL (A BOUQUET OF THE HERB STALKS)
SALT
PEPPER
OIL FOR BAGS AND PAN
1 CUP DRY WHITE VERMOUTH

Sauce:
1 HANDFUL FRESH TARRAGON OR 2 TO 3 TEASPOONS DRIED TARRAGON
1 CUP DRY WHITE VERMOUTH
1 CUP WHIPPING CREAM
½ POUND (2 STICKS) BUTTER

1. Stuff the fish with the dried fennel. Sprinkle with salt and pepper. Oil a small brown paper bag. (You may make your own from waxed paper, parchment paper or aluminum foil rather than using a paper bag for each fish.) Oil a pan large enough to hold all the bags. Place the fish and the dried fennel in each bag. Pour ¼ cup of the vermouth in each bag and carefully seal the end of the bags by folding tightly three times.

2. Preheat the oven to 450 F. Place the bags on the oiled pan, seam side up, and bake for 15 minutes until the bags puff up. For a dinner party you may put the fish in the bags ahead of time and add the vermouth just before you put them in the oven.

3. To make the sauce, place the tarragon in a pan with one cup of dry white vermouth. Boil until it is reduced to a glaze. (Be careful not to evaporate all the wine!) Add the cup of cream and boil again, reducing it to ½ cup of liquid in all. Whisk the cream from time to time. Use a pan that is high enough so that the cream won't boil over, or use one of the new "gadgets" that prevents this.

4. As soon as the cream is reduced to ½ cup, remove the pan from the heat. Cool slightly. Add the butter, whisking as you add it. Strain the sauce into a sauceboat.

5. Slit the bags at the table and add a bit of sauce to each serving.

GRILLED SALMON WITH SHALLOT BUTTER

Raymond Sokolov

6 servings

⅔ CUP SHALLOTS, CHOPPED
8 TABLESPOONS (1 STICK) BUTTER,
  MELTED
6 SALMON STEAKS
OIL FOR PAINTING THE BROILER

1. Blanch the shallots in plenty of simmering, lightly salted water for 5 minutes. Drain and purée them in a blender with melted butter. Collect the shallot butter, while butter is still pourable, into a glass or metal container that can serve as a mold (if you want to serve the butter cold) or into a saucepan (if you want to pour the butter over the salmon as a hot sauce).

2. Preheat the broiler or prepare a charcoal fire.

3. Grill the steaks 2 inches from the broiler or 2 inches above the charcoal bed on an oiled grill.

4. Turn the steaks carefully after 5 minutes. Cook another 5 minutes, or until the flesh just turns flaky.

5. Serve immediately. Pass the sauce separately, either hot from a sauceboat or as a solid butter that can be sliced onto the fish and allowed to melt.

SWEET AND SOUR WHOLE FISH

Paula J. Buchholz

6 servings

You can deep-fry any of the following kinds of fish: rock cod, bluefish, carp, halibut, mackerel, red snapper, sea bass, trout or whitefish.

Sauce:
½ CUP SUGAR
½ CUP VINEGAR
⅓ CUP PINEAPPLE JUICE
3 TABLESPOONS CATSUP
2 TABLESPOONS SALAD OIL
1 TABLESPOON SOY SAUCE
2 TABLESPOONS CORNSTARCH
  DISSOLVED IN 2 TABLESPOONS
  COLD WATER
1 SMALL ONION, THINLY SLICED
½ GREEN PEPPER, THINLY SLICED
1 MEDIUM-SIZED TOMATO, CUT IN
  THIN WEDGES

1 TEASPOON FINELY MINCED
  FRESH GINGER

Other Ingredients:
1 WHOLE FISH (ABOUT 3 POUNDS),
  CLEANED AND SCALED
1 EGG, BEATEN
1 TEASPOON SOY SAUCE
½ TEASPOON SALT
CORNSTARCH
OIL FOR DEEP-FRYING

1. To prepare the sauce, mix the following ingredients together in a wok or

skillet: the sugar, vinegar, pineapple juice, catsup, salad oil and 1 tablespoon soy sauce. Bring the mixture to a boil, stirring to blend well. Then gradually stir in the dissolved cornstarch. When the sauce is thickened and smooth, add the onion, green pepper, tomato and ginger. Heat through before serving.

2. Coat the whole fish with a mixture of beaten egg combined with 1 teaspoon soy sauce and the salt. Then roll it in cornstarch.

3. Fill a wok or deep skillet with enough oil to deep-fry the fish. When the oil is heated to 375 F., add the fish and deep-fry it until browned (about 15 minutes). Remove the fish from the oil and drain on absorbent toweling.

4. Pour the sauce over the fish to serve.

BAKED BLUEFISH WITH CLAMS

Florence Fabricant

4 servings

1 2-POUND BLUEFISH, CLEANED
  AND LEFT WHOLE
12 LITTLENECK CLAMS
1 TEASPOON DRIED OREGANO
½ TEASPOON DRIED ROSEMARY
SALT
FRESHLY GROUND BLACK PEPPER
6 TABLESPOONS OLIVE OIL
JUICE OF 1 LEMON
1 CLOVE GARLIC, MINCED
1 TABLESPOON FINELY CHOPPED
  SCALLIONS
1 TABLESPOON MINCED FRESH
  PARSLEY

1. Preheat the oven to 450 F. Wipe the bluefish dry, inside and out. Scrub the clams and set aside.

2. Mix the oregano and rosemary together. Make three or four diagonal slashes about one-half-inch deep on each side of the fish. Rub the herbs into the slashes and into the body cavity. Season the fish with salt and pepper.

3. Spread 1 tablespoon of the olive oil in an oblong baking pan. Place the fish in the pan. Mix 4 tablespoons of the oil with the lemon juice and pour it over the fish, sprinkling some into the body cavity as well: Spread the garlic and scallions in the pan and arrange the clams around the fish.

4. Bake for 20 to 25 minutes, basting the fish after 10 minutes. The dish is done when the fish can be easily separated from the bone and the clams have opened.

5. Sprinkle the fish and clams with parsley and serve, basting each serving with the pan juices.

RED SNAPPER BAKED IN VERMOUTH
AND ORANGE JUICE

Maurice Moore-Betty

8 servings

3 TO 4 POUNDS WHOLE RED
  SNAPPER
FLOUR, LIGHTLY SEASONED WITH
  SALT AND PEPPER
8 TABLESPOONS (1 STICK) BUTTER
1 CUP ORANGE JUICE
1 CUP DRY WHITE VERMOUTH
SALT
PEPPER
4 ORANGES, CUT IN SLICES OR
  WEDGES
WATERCRESS FOR GARNISH

1. Preheat the oven to 450 F.

2. Prepare the snapper for cooking: scrape off the scales and season it inside and out with seasoned flour. Leave the head and tail on.

3. Melt the butter in a baking pan. Add the orange juice and dry vermouth. Bring to a boil and simmer for 2 to 3 minutes. Lay the fish in the pan and baste it with the orange juice mixture.

4. Bake uncovered for 30 to 35 minutes, basting thoroughly and frequently. Test for doneness.

5. Remove to a serving platter. Reduce the pan juices and pour them over the fish. Adjust seasoning with salt and pepper. Garnish with orange slices or wedges and watercress.

MARINATED FISH PROVENÇAL

Carol Cutler

6 servings

Sauce:
1 CUP TOMATO SAUCE
½ CUP VINEGAR
½ CUP DRY WHITE WINE
¼ CUP OLIVE OIL
1 TEASPOON ROSEMARY
1 TEASPOON SUGAR
PINCH OF SAFFRON
3 GARLIC CLOVES, MASHED
PIECE OF ORANGE RIND, ABOUT
  1-INCH SQUARE

Other Ingredients:
OIL FOR FRYING
1 CUP FLOUR (APPROXIMATELY)
3 POUNDS FISH—HALIBUT,
  HADDOCK OR COD, CUT INTO
  1-INCH-THICK SLICES
SALT
PEPPER

28

1. Put all the sauce ingredients in a small pot, cover, and simmer for 20 minutes.

2. While the sauce simmers, pour the oil into a skillet to a depth of about ½-inch and heat until you can see the heat waves.

3. Flour the fish slices and fry them quickly in oil; turn to brown both sides. Fry the fish 1 to 2 minutes per side, depending on thickness.

4. Remove the fried fish to a deep dish large enough to hold the hot sauce as well. Sprinkle salt and pepper over the fish.

5. Pour the simmering sauce over the slices. Cover at once and let cool at room temperature. Refrigerate at least 24 hours.

6. To serve, lift a whole fillet onto each individual dish and cover it liberally with sauce. Pass crusty french bread to absorb the extra sauce.

FISH WITH CAPERS (PESCE AI CAPPERI)

Giuliano Bugialli

4 servings

In Italy, the large Mediterranean fish *San Pietro*, or *Palombo*, is used for this dish. The large Atlantic fish suggested below may be substituted. Since we never get fresh cod in Italy, for us it remains a treat, though Americans may get less excited about it. Capers grow all over Italy in the crumbling antique walls; their white flowers are a beautiful sight in June and July.

4 SLICES (ABOUT 2 POUNDS) OF A LARGE FISH SUCH AS HADDOCK, HALIBUT, STRIPED BASS OR FRESH COD
1 CUP COLD MILK
1 CUP FLOUR
5 TABLESPOONS BUTTER
4 TABLESPOONS OLIVE OIL

2 TABLESPOONS COARSELY CHOPPED CAPERS IN WINE VINEGAR
1 TABLESPOON FINELY CHOPPED ITALIAN PARSLEY PLUS 4 WHOLE SPRIGS PARSLEY
SALT
FRESHLY GROUND BLACK PEPPER

1. Soak the fish slices in cold milk for about 30 minutes.

2. Remove the fish slices from the milk and pat them dry with paper towels.

3. Lightly flour the fish slices and let them stand for 5 minutes on paper towels.

4. Place a large frying pan over heat with 2 tablespoons of the butter and the olive oil. When the butter is melted, sauté the fish slices for about 5 minutes on each side, sprinkling them with salt and freshly ground pepper.

5. Remove the pan from the heat and transfer the fish slices to a serving dish.

6. Place a saucepan over heat and add the remaining 3 tablespoons of butter. When the butter is completely melted, remove the pan from the heat and add the chopped capers. Stir the sauce very well with a wooden spoon and pour it over the fish slices. Sprinkle with chopped parsley and place one sprig of parsley on each fish slice. Serve immediately.

BAKED SHAD ROE

Helen McCully

4 servings

16 TABLESPOONS (2 STICKS)
  BUTTER
¾ CUP CHOPPED PARSLEY
4 PAIRS SHAD ROE
SALT
FRESHLY GROUND PEPPER
½ CUP DRY WHITE WINE

1. Cut four rectangles of foil, each large enough to encompass a pair of roe, envelope-fashion. Spread 3 tablespoons butter over the center of each piece of foil, sprinkle with 3 tablespoons finely chopped parsley. Place a pair of roe on top, dot with 1 tablespoon butter and salt and pepper them lightly.

2. Pull the foil up at the ends, then add about 2 tablespoons of dry white wine to each packet. Close the foil and seal it so that the liquids won't escape.

3. Bake in a preheated 350 F. oven for 20 minutes.

4. To serve, lift the roe from the foil to hot plates along with the juices. (Serve with garlic-flavored mashed potatoes and lemon wedges. A bottle of good dry white wine should accompany this dish.)

SPICY FISH AND CORN CHOWDER

Jeanne Lesem

2 servings

2 SLICES BACON
1 SMALL WHITE ONION, MINCED
1 8-OUNCE CAN TOMATOES
1⅓ CUPS WATER
½ TO ¾ POUND BONELESS FISH
  SUCH AS COD, HADDOCK OR
  POLLOCK, CUT IN BITE-SIZED
  CHUNKS
1 SMALL GREEN PEPPER, SEEDED
AND FINELY CHOPPED
1 8-OUNCE CAN CREAM-STYLE
  CORN
½ TEASPOON SALT
½ TEASPOON CHILI POWDER
PINCH CELERY SEED
1 TABLESPOON BUTTER
1 TABLESPOON FLOUR

1. Dice the bacon and place it in a 2½-quart saucepan over low heat and cook, turning as needed to brown the bacon evenly.

2. When the bacon is crisp, remove it with a slotted spoon to drain on paper toweling.

3. Add the onion to the bacon fat and cook, stirring, until the onion softens slightly and starts to brown.

4. Add the tomatoes, their juice and the water and simmer five minutes.

5. Add the fish and green pepper; simmer another five minutes, until the fish has lost its opacity and flakes when poked gently with a fork.

6. Add the corn, salt, chili powder and celery seed. Stir to mix and let simmer while you cream the butter with flour to make a thickener.

7. Add butter-flour mixture in bits, stirring, until it melts and the chowder thickens slightly.

8. Serve at once or quick-cool by setting the pan in cold water and stirring the contents. When cool, pour into a storage container that can be tightly covered and refrigerate overnight. Reheat slowly over low heat, stirring often.

SWORDFISH OR SHARK STEAKS GRILLED IN LETTUCE LEAVES

Carole Lalli

4 servings

1½ TO 2 POUNDS FRESH SWORD-
  FISH OR SHARK STEAKS,
  DIVIDED INTO FOUR PORTIONS
ENOUGH BOSTON OR LEAF
  LETTUCE TO WRAP UP THE FISH

Marinade:
JUICE OF 1 LEMON
4 TABLESPOONS OLIVE OIL
2 TABLESPOONS FENNEL SEEDS
½ TEASPOON SALT
2 OR MORE CLOVES GARLIC,
  MINCED
2 TABLESPOONS ITALIAN OR
  CURLY PARSLEY

1. Marinate the fish in the marinade for several hours at least; all day or overnight is even better.

2. Make a charcoal fire in an outdoor grill or in a hibachi.

3. Spread the lettuce leaves flat and lift the fish onto them, keeping a fair amount of marinade on each piece. Dribble some more on top. Cover the fish with more leaves and tie it with kitchen string. If you like, place the fish packets in a hinged grilling basket that will hold them snugly.

4. Grill the fish over white hot coals for about 10 minutes on each side, depending on the thickness of the steaks.

Note: For even more aromatic flavor, toss on an additional handful of fennel seeds, or, if available, place some dried fennel branches over the coals just before putting on the fish.

BAKED JAPANESE-STYLE SALMON
ON PINE NEEDLES (MATSUBA-YAKI)

Toshio Morimoto

4 servings

COARSE SALT
PINE NEEDLES SUFFICIENT TO
  COVER BOTTOM OF 12-INCH
  ROUND CASSEROLE
4 4-OUNCE SALMON FILLETS
8 JAPANESE DRIED MUSHROOMS,
  SOAKED OVERNIGHT
12 CHESTNUTS, ROASTED AND
  PEELED (OR SUBSTITUTE
  CANNED)

Sauce:
4 TABLESPOONS FINELY
  GRATED WHITE RADISH
4 TEASPOONS SOY SAUCE
¼ TEASPOON MONOSODIUM
  GLUTAMATE (OPTIONAL)
⅓ CUP JAPANESE SOUP STOCK
  (DASHI, AVAILABLE DRIED, IN
  PACKETS, IN ORIENTAL GROCERY
  STORES)

1. Place a layer of salt into a 12-inch-round flameproof earthenware casserole
   with a tight-fitting lid. Sprinkle the salt lightly with water and spread a layer of
   pine needles over the salt to cover it completely.

2. Place the salmon fillets on the pine needles and salt them lightly. Spread the
   mushrooms and chestnuts over the fish and cover the casserole.

3. Place the casserole over medium heat and let it "steam-bake" for 15 minutes.

4. Meanwhile make the dipping sauce by combining the sauce ingredients.

5. Serve the salmon directly from the casserole and accompany it with the
   dipping sauce in small individual bowls.

BAKED MACKEREL OR SHAD FILLETS
WITH MUSTARD MAYONNAISE SAUCE

Jeanne Lesem

2 servings

Sauce:
¼ CUP MAYONNAISE, PREFERABLY
  HOMEMADE
¼ CUP MOCK CRÈME FRAÎCHE
  (SEE PAGE 37)
1½ TEASPOONS TO 1 TABLESPOON
  MUSTARD, DIJON- OR CREOLE-
  STYLE

⅛ TEASPOON MINCED FRESH
  GARLIC (OPTIONAL)

Other Ingredients:
¾ TO 1 POUND BONED MACKEREL
  OR SHAD FILLETS
SALAD OR COOKING OIL

1. First prepare the sauce. Stir the mayonnaise, mock crème fraîche, mustard
   and garlic (if you are using it) together in a small bowl until smoothly
   blended. Serve cold or at room temperature or set the bowl in a skillet of hot,
   but not boiling, water over lowest possible heat and stir constantly until the
   sauce is warm. Do not let it get really hot or the mayonnaise may make it

curdle. Curdling does not affect the flavor, but the texture is unattractive.

2. Preheat the oven to 450 F.

3. Choose a baking pan or dish just large enough to hold the fillets in a single layer. Oil it only if fillets have been skinned. (If not, the skin should stick to the pan when you remove the cooked fish; a spatula or pancake turner will slide easily between the flesh and skin of the cooked fillets.)

4. Place the fillets (skin side down) in the pan and brush them lightly with oil.

5. Measure the fillets at their thickest point. Place them on the middle shelf of the oven and bake 10 minutes for each inch of thickness. If one end of a fillet is very thin, tuck it under before baking to cook more evenly. Baking time may have to be extended slightly if fillets were very cold when put into the oven or if the baking dish is ovenproof glass or ceramic; both take longer to heat than metal. The fish is done when it has lost its opacity and it separates into flakes when poked gently with a fork.

6. Serve directly from the baking pan or dish at the table. Pass the sauce separately.

PICKLED FISH FILLETS WITH PEPPERS, ONIONS AND CARROTS

Elizabeth Colchie

6 servings

2 CUPS SLICED ONIONS
1½ CUPS THINLY SLICED CARROTS
½ CUP THINLY SLICED RED BELL PEPPER
½ CUP THINLY SLICED GREEN BELL PEPPER
2 SLICED GARLIC CLOVES
1 TEASPOON CORIANDER SEEDS
½ TEASPOON PEPPERCORNS
2 CRUMBLED BAY LEAVES
¼ TEASPOON ALLSPICE BERRIES

¾ CUP OLIVE OIL
⅔ CUP DRY WHITE WINE
½ CUP WHITE WINE VINEGAR
2 TEASPOONS SALT
2 POUNDS (APPROXIMATELY) THICK, FIRM-FLESHED FISH FILLETS OR STEAKS (SHAD OR KING MACKEREL WORK WELL), CUT INTO ABOUT 12 NEAT PIECES
2 TABLESPOONS LIME JUICE
LIME SLIVERS FOR GARNISH

1. In a skillet, cook the onions, carrots, peppers, garlic, coriander, peppercorns, bay leaves, and allspice in olive oil for about 10 minutes over moderately low heat. Add the wine, vinegar and salt and barely simmer, covered, for 5 minutes.

2. Arrange the fish, skin side down, in a large oiled baking dish; sprinkle it with lime juice and let it stand a few minutes.

3. Pour on the hot vegetable mixture; bake at 350 F. for 20 minutes, or until the fish just flakes easily. (If you have used a fish with skin, remove it.) Let cool.

4. Garnish with slivers of lime and chill for 12 to 24 hours before serving. Remove from the refrigerator 30 minutes before serving.

SWORDFISH MEDALLIONS WITH VERMOUTH

Nicola Zanghi

6 servings

2½ POUNDS SWORDFISH SLICED INTO ¼-INCH-THICK MEDALLIONS, APPROXIMATELY 4 INCHES SQUARE
FLOUR FOR DREDGING
VEGETABLE OIL
½ CUP CLARIFIED BUTTER
1 TABLESPOON CHOPPED SHALLOTS

⅔ CUP DRY VERMOUTH
JUICE OF 1 LEMON
DASH OF WORCESTERSHIRE SAUCE
SALT
FRESHLY GROUND PEPPER
2 TABLESPOONS CHOPPED FRESH PARSLEY
2 TABLESPOONS BUTTER AT ROOM TEMPERATURE

1. Lightly flour each medallion.

2. Heat the oil and clarified butter until a light haze forms over it. Over a high flame, sauté each medallion until lightly browned on each side.

3. Transfer the fish to a warmed serving platter and keep hot.

4. Discard all but 1 tablespoon of the butter-oil mixture; lower the heat to medium, add the shallots and cook until transparent.

5. Add the vermouth and lemon juice and reduce by half.

6. Add the Worcestershire sauce, salt (approximately ⅛ teaspoon), pepper, parsley and butter to the skillet; over a high flame swirl the skillet until the butter melts into the sauce. Pour the sauce over the fish.

COLD SHAD WITH DILL AND MUSTARD SAUCE

Elizabeth Colchie

6 servings

2¼ CUPS WATER
¾ CUP DRY WHITE WINE
⅓ CUP LEMON JUICE
¼ CUP FRESH DILL, SNIPPED
1 TEASPOON CRUSHED WHITE PEPPERCORNS
1 TEASPOON SALT
3 1-POUND SHAD FILLETS
2 EGG YOLKS

1½ TABLESPOONS DIJON-STYLE MUSTARD
2 TEASPOONS SUGAR
¼ TEASPOON SALT
¼ TEASPOON WHITE PEPPER
⅓ CUP PEANUT OIL
⅔ CUP OLIVE OIL
1 TO 2 TABLESPOONS FINELY CUT DILL

1. In a large enamel or stainless skillet combine the water, wine, lemon juice, snipped dill, peppercorns and salt. Simmer for a few minutes, then add the fish and cook, covered, at a bare simmer, for 8 to 10 minutes, or until the fish flakes easily when pulled with a fork. Cool the fish in the poaching liquid. Refrigerate for an hour or longer.

2. In a small bowl, combine the egg yolks, mustard, sugar, ¼ teaspoon each of salt and white pepper and beat with a whisk until frothy. Add the peanut oil very gradually, whisking constantly until it is well incorporated. Add the olive oil gradually, whisking constantly. Add dill to taste, and check the seasoning.

3. Place the chilled fish fillets on paper towels to blot excess liquid. Arrange them on a serving platter. Spoon some of the sauce over the fish and serve the rest separately.

TURBOT WITH MOUSSELINE SAUCE

Joanne Will

8 servings

Sauce:
3 EGG YOLKS
3 TABLESPOONS WHIPPING CREAM
½ CLOVE GARLIC, MASHED
½ TEASPOON SALT
¼ TEASPOON DRY MUSTARD
3 TABLESPOONS LEMON JUICE
12 TABLESPOONS (1½ STICKS) BUTTER
1 CUP MINCED MUSHROOMS, SAUTÉED IN ADDITIONAL BUTTER AND WELL DRAINED
1 TABLESPOON MINCED PARSLEY
1 TABLESPOON MINCED CHIVES

1 TEASPOON DRY TARRAGON, CRUSHED
½ CUP WHIPPING CREAM

Other Ingredients:
1 WHOLE TURBOT OR TURBOT FILLETS (3 TO 4 POUNDS)
SALT
WHITE PEPPER
¼ CUP MELTED BUTTER
MINCED PARSLEY FOR GARNISH
LEMON WEDGES FOR GARNISH

1. Whisk the egg yolks in a pottery bowl or the top of a glass or porcelain-lined double boiler. Whisk in the 3 tablespoons whipping cream, garlic, salt, dry mustard and lemon juice. Set the bowl over a saucepan of boiling water, or in the top of a double boiler. The bowl or pan should be 2 inches above boiling water.

2. Cook on low heat, beating constantly, until the mixture has the consistency of thick cream. Remove the bowl or pan from the heat and whisk in the butter, about 2 tablespoons at a time. Whisk constantly until the butter is blended. Cool the sauce slightly.

3. Fold the mushrooms, parsley, chives and tarragon into the sauce. Whip the cream and fold it into the sauce.

4. Wipe the turbot or turbot fillets with a damp cloth. Pat dry with paper towels. Place the fish skin side down on buttered heavy foil in a broiler pan. Season with salt and pepper. Brush it with melted butter. Put the pan under a pre-heated broiler, 3 to 4 inches from the heat source. Broil 10 minutes, or until the fish flakes easily with a fork. (If you prefer, the fish may be oven-poached in court bouillon, covered with foil, for about 15 minutes at 375 F.)

5. Serve the sauce with the fish. Garnish the fish with more minced parsley and lemon wedges.

MACKEREL PÂTÉ

Paula J. Buchholz

3 cups

1 SMALL ONION, FINELY MINCED
3 TABLESPOONS BUTTER
1 CAN (15 OUNCES) MACKEREL,
  DRAINED
¼ TEASPOON ALLSPICE
¼ TEASPOON MACE
¼ TEASPOON FRESHLY GROUND
  BLACK PEPPER
¼ TEASPOON SALT
¼ TEASPOON THYME
⅓ CUP BRANDY
8 TABLESPOONS (1 STICK) BUTTER
1 PACKAGE (3 OUNCES) CREAM
  CHEESE
1 TABLESPOON LEMON JUICE

1. Cook the onions slowly in 3 tablespoons butter until tender, but not brown (about 15 minutes). Add the mackerel, allspice, mace, pepper, salt and thyme. Cook over high heat, stirring constantly, for a minute or two. Pour on the brandy. Ignite with a lighted match. Let burn 1 minute, then extinguish the flames by covering the skillet and removing it from the heat.

2. Purée the mixture in a blender or food processor until smooth. Then beat in the 8 tablespoons butter, cream cheese and lemon juice.

3. Pack into a jar or crock and refrigerate at least 2 hours before serving.

4. Serve as a spread with squares of toast.

Note: If you like, substitute 1 pound of cooked fresh fish for the canned mackerel.

BAKED FISH WITH CREAMY GREEN PEPPERCORN SAUCE

Jeanne Lesem

4 servings

This recipe and the one on page 32 call for mock *crème fraîche* (following). Make the *crème fraîche* at least a day in advance of preparing either dish.

¾ TO 1 POUND FISH STEAKS OR
  FILLETS: ANY LEAN, WHITE-
  FLESHED FRESH OR SALTWATER
  FISH, SUCH AS CATFISH, COD,
  CUSK, HADDOCK, HALIBUT,
  POLLOCK, SEA TROUT (KNOWN
  AS WEAKFISH IN SOME AREAS)
  OR WHITING
SALAD OIL

1. Preheat the oven to 450 F.

2. Place the fish (skin side down if the skin is still on) in a pan or shallow baking dish just large enough to hold them in a single layer. If you are using fillets with the skin on, do not oil the pan or dish; the skin will stick to the pan making it easy to separate the meat from it with a spatula after cooking.

3. Lightly oil the fish, place it on the middle shelf of the oven, and bake uncovered 10 minutes for every inch of thickness (measure the fish at its thickest point). If a fillet tapers to a very thin point, fold that end under so it will cook evenly.

Sauce:
1 MEDIUM EGG YOLK
⅛ TEASPOON SALT
1 TO 2 TEASPOONS FRESH LEMON
  JUICE
½ CUP (½ STICK) BUTTER,
  MELTED AND COOLED
¼ CUP MOCK *CRÈME FRAÎCHE*
  (FOLLOWING)
1 TEASPOON GREEN PEPPERCORNS
  IN BRINE, DRAINED, RINSED AND
  DRAINED AGAIN, OR FREEZE-
  DRIED GREEN PEPPERCORNS

1. While the fish cooks, prepare the sauce. However, if you are using thin fillets that will bake quickly, make the sauce in advance. Rinse a 1-pint, non-aluminum mixing bowl with very hot, but not boiling, water. Place the egg yolk, salt and 1 teaspoon of the lemon juice in a bowl. Beat until the yolk is smooth and a light lemon color. Begin adding the melted butter by drops, beating constantly. When the mixture thickens perceptibly, add the remaining butter at a slightly faster speed until all of it is incorporated. Stop occasionally to scrape down the sides of the bowl with a rubber scraper.

2. Stir in the mock *crème fraîche* until no streaks show.

3. Crush the peppercorns coarsely with a mortar and pestle, stir them in, and serve the sauce at once with the fish, or set the bowl in a shallow pan of hot, but not boiling, water to keep it warm. Stir occasionally if it is to be held for longer than 15 to 20 minutes. (This sauce can be reheated successfully in a glass or china container by setting it in a pan of hot, but not boiling, water over the lowest possible heat, and stirring constantly with a spoon, rubber scraper or wire whisk until the sauce is barely warm.)

Mock Crème Fraîche:
This slightly tart cream approximates the thick *crème fraîche* served in France.

1 CUP HEAVY CREAM, NOT
  ULTRA-PASTEURIZED*
1 TABLESPOON BUTTERMILK, PLAIN
  YOGURT OR DAIRY SOUR CREAM

1. Pour the cream into a 12-ounce glass jar with a tight-fitting lid. Gently stir in the buttermilk, yogurt or sour cream. Cover the jar loosely with cheesecloth or a paper towel and let it stand at room temperature until the mixture thickens. This can take up to 12 hours in a very cool room, or as little as 5 to 8 hours in a warm room.

Continued from preceding page

2. When the mixture is very thick, remove the cheesecloth or paper towel, cover the jar tightly with its lid, and refrigerate until well chilled. The cream will keep at least one month if, after every use, you return the container to the refrigerator as soon as you have measured out the amount you want. If it separates during long storage, simply stir it before measuring out what you need. Mock *crème fraîche* can be used in cold or hot sauces, but it is most useful in hot ones ·because, unlike dairy sour cream or yogurt, it does not · curdle when boiled.

* Mock *crème fraîche* can be made with light or heavy ultra-pasteurized cream, but the results will have an unpleasant, cooked flavor.

POACHED RED SNAPPER OR CARP IN ASPIC WITH GREEN MAYONNAISE SAUCE

Paul Rubinstein

4 to 6 servings

1 4-POUND RED SNAPPER OR CARP, CLEANED
2 MEDIUM-SIZED ONIONS, SLICED
2 CARROTS, SLICED
2 STALKS CELERY WITH LEAVES, SLICED
1 BAY LEAF
4 8-OUNCE BOTTLES CLAM JUICE
1 CUP DRY WHITE WINE
2 ENVELOPES UNFLAVORED GELATIN

Sauce:
1½ CUPS MAYONNAISE
1 TEASPOON CHOPPED PARSLEY
1 TEASPOON CHOPPED TARRAGON LEAVES
4 DROPS GREEN FOOD COLORING
1 TABLESPOON LEMON JUICE
2 TEASPOONS WORCESTERSHIRE SAUCE
½ TEASPOON SALT

1. Preheat the oven to 350 F.

2. Place the red snapper or carp in a fish poacher, add the onions, carrots, celery, bay leaf, clam juice and wine.

3. Cover the poacher and place it on the middle rack of the preheated oven for 1 hour. When done, lift out the fish on the tray of the fish poacher and transfer it to a wooden board or tray.

4. Pour the liquid together with the vegetables from the poacher into a saucepan and set aside.

5. When the fish has cooled, remove the head and tail and add them to the saucepan with the liquid. Then carefully separate the meat from the bones and skin. Add the bones to the saucepan, and refrigerate the fish.

6. Bring the liquid to a boil, reduce the heat, cover and simmer gently for 15 minutes. Meanwhile dissolve the gelatin in about ½ cup warm water.

7. Strain the liquid through a fine strainer lined with cheesecloth, then add the softened gelatin to the strained liquid, bring to a simmer again and turn off the heat.

8. Into a 3-quart ring mold, or a mold in the form of a fish or other decorative shape of about the same capacity, pour enough liquid to cover the bottom by ⅛ to ¼ inch. Refrigerate until it jells.

9. Arrange the pieces of boned snapper or carp evenly in the mold, fill with the remaining liquid, and refrigerate for several hours.

10. While the aspic is jelling, combine the mayonnaise, parsley, tarragon, food coloring, lemon juice, Worcestershire sauce and salt in a mixing bowl and mix well, making sure the color is even. Transfer to a sauceboat and refrigerate.

11. To serve, unmold the snapper or carp in aspic by quickly dipping the mold in very hot water then reversing it onto a serving platter. Serve with the mayonnaise sauce.

TROUT WITH RIESLING WINE SAUCE
(TRUITES AU RIESLING)

Nicola Zanghi

4 servings

4 10- TO 12-OUNCE BONELESS
  WHOLE TROUT
FLOUR FOR DREDGING
MILK FOR DIPPING
½ CUP VEGETABLE OIL
½ CUP CLARIFIED BUTTER
SALT
FRESHLY GROUND PEPPER

Sauce:
1 CUP RIESLING
2 CUPS SOUR CREAM
1 TABLESPOON FRESH TARRAGON
  OR SUBSTITUTE 1½ TEASPOONS
  DRIED
WORCESTERSHIRE SAUCE
LEMON JUICE
4 TABLESPOONS BUTTER, AT ROOM
  TEMPERATURE
2 EGG YOLKS, WELL BEATEN
NUTMEG

1. Pat the trout dry. Dredge it in flour, dip it in milk, then dredge it in flour again.

2. Heat the oil and clarified butter until a light haze forms over it. Add the fish and sauté until it is golden brown on both sides, turning twice. Season with salt and freshly ground pepper. Transfer the fish to a warm serving platter and keep it in a warm oven.

3. Prepare the sauce by draining off excess oil from the skillet. Add the wine and reduce it to ⅓ cup. Lower the heat to moderate; scrape the pan with a wooden spoon.

4. Add the sour cream, tarragon, a dash of Worcestershire and a few drops of lemon juice and swirl the pan until the sauce is warmed through.

5. Over low heat, add the butter and mix in the egg yolks, being careful not to allow the sauce to boil. Dust with nutmeg, stir and adjust the seasoning if necessary. Pour the sauce over the fish.

TROUT WITH LEMON-BUTTER

Nathalie Dupree

4 servings

4 RAINBOW TROUT, WITH HEADS
   ON
¼ CUP FLOUR, SEASONED WITH
   SALT AND PEPPER
3 TABLESPOONS CLARIFIED BUTTER
   OR BUTTER AND OIL, MIXED

SALT
PEPPER
1 TABLESPOON CHOPPED PARSLEY
1 TEASPOON CHOPPED FRESH
   HERBS (CHIVES, THYME)

Sauce:
3 TABLESPOONS BUTTER
JUICE OF ½ LEMON

1. Wash and clean the trout. Cut off the fins. Trim the tails in a neat "V." Pat the fish dry with paper towels. Roll them in the seasoned flour.

2. Heat a heavy frying pan. When it is hot, add the 3 tablespoons butter or butter and oil. When it foams, quickly put in the floured fish and cook over medium heat until it is golden brown on both sides, turning once. Cook 5 to 6 minutes on each side or 10 minutes total for each inch of thickness, measured at the thickest point. Do not put all the fish in at one time, as that will reduce the heat in the pan and your fish will not cook fast enough. If necessary, do each fish individually and keep warm in the oven.

3. Place the cooked trout on a hot platter.

4. Wipe out the pan, add butter and cook to a hazelnut-brown color. Add the lemon juice, salt and pepper, parsley and other herbs and pour the butter, foaming, over the trout. Serve at once.

QUICK-BAKED RED SNAPPER

Harvey Steiman

4 servings

4 SNAPPER FILLETS,* 5 TO 6
   OUNCES EACH
¼ CUP DRY BREAD CRUMBS
SALT
PEPPER
6 TABLESPOONS (¾ STICK)
   BUTTER
½ MEDIUM-SIZED ONION, SLICED
1 CLOVE GARLIC, CRUSHED
JUICE OF 1 LEMON

1. Preheat the oven to 450 F.

2. Coat a flat baking dish with butter or oil. Arrange the fish skin side down.

Cover evenly with bread crumbs. Salt and pepper to taste.

3. Melt the butter in a small skillet or saucepan. Simmer the onion and garlic in butter over moderate heat until they begin to brown slightly, then squeeze on the lemon juice, swirl the mixture for 10 to 15 seconds, or until steam subsides, and pour it evenly over the fish.

4. Bake 5 to 10 minutes, depending on the thickness of the fish.

   * Any firm, white-fleshed fish may be substituted for snapper, as long as it is no thicker than ¾-inch.

SAND DABS WITH MUSHROOMS

Harvey Steiman

4 to 6 servings

This was an improvisation I came up with to serve my Boston aunt when I was visiting her in California, hence the sand dabs. You can substitute any light-fleshed fish for the sand dabs.

The postscript is that later that week, when we were dining at a Mexican restaurant, one of the daily specials was sand dabs with mushroom-and-wine sauce. What I can't figure out is how they found out about it so fast!

Sauce:
3 TABLESPOONS BUTTER
¾ POUND FRESH MUSHROOMS, SLICED
2 SHALLOTS, FINELY CHOPPED
½ CUP WHITE WINE
1 CUP CREAM
2 TABLESPOONS CHOPPED PARSLEY
JUICE OF 1 LEMON
SALT
PEPPER

Other Ingredients:
2 MEDIUM ONIONS, THINLY SLICED
2 POUNDS FLAT FISH (SAND DAB, TROUT, SOLE, FLOUNDER) FILLETS
1 CUP WHITE WINE
SALT
PEPPER

1. Begin the sauce by melting the butter over moderately high heat. Sauté the mushrooms until they start to give up their juices.

2. Add the shallots and wine to the mushrooms and boil for 1 minute. Add the cream, reduce the heat and simmer, stirring, 2 to 3 minutes, until the cream thickens somewhat. Add the parsley and lemon juice. Salt and pepper to taste.

3. Preheat the oven to 400 F.

4. Arrange the onions to cover the bottom of a large baking pan. Lay the fish on top of the onions without overlapping. Pour in the wine. Season the fish with salt and pepper. Bring to a simmer over moderate heat, cover with foil and bake 5 to 10 minutes, or until the fish is opaque all the way through.

5. When the fish is done, lift the pieces with a slotted spoon onto a heated serving platter. Spoon the mushroom sauce over the fish and serve.

Shellfish

SQUID IN WINE SAUCE WITH ROSEMARY (KALAMARAKIA KRASATA)

Vilma Liacouras Chantiles

4 servings

Squid are mollusks, beloved by Hellenes and Italians since ancient times. They are also enjoyed by Oriental peoples as well as Central and South Americans. Your sauce will be richly colored if you include a few of the tiny, inky sacs found inside the squid bodies.

1 POUND SQUID, SMALL IF POSSIBLE (LONG FINGER-LENGTHS)
SALT
4 TABLESPOONS VEGETABLE OIL
1 SMALL ONION, 2 SHALLOTS, OR 4 SCALLIONS, CHOPPED
1¼ CUPS FRESH OR CANNED TOMATOES

½ CUP TOMATO JUICE
⅓ CUP DRY RED OR WHITE WINE
2 TO 3 CLOVES GARLIC, MINCED
1 BAY LEAF
LARGE SPRIG FRESH ROSEMARY OR 1½ TEASPOONS DRIED ROSEMARY
SALT
FRESHLY GROUND PEPPER

1. Wash the squid and salt them slightly. Let them sit for 10 to 15 minutes.

2. To clean, rub the bodies and tentacles under cold running water until the outer, flecked skin can be peeled off. Separate the bodies from the heads (including the 10 arms or tentacles). Cut off and discard the eye section of the heads. Squeeze out the small shell under the tentacles and discard it. Reserve the tentacles. Squeeze out the contents of the bodies and pull out the cartilaginous support (it looks like a clear "spine"). The inky sacs may be saved, or discarded with the innards. Slice the bodies into circles and chop the tentacles or leave whole, as you wish. Drain.

3. To make the sauce, heat the oil and in it sauté the onion, shallots or scallions. Stir in the tomatoes and juice, wine, garlic, bay leaf and rosemary. Simmer 5 minutes. Season with salt and pepper.

4. Add the squid. Cover tightly and simmer over minimum heat 1 hour until tender, or transfer the mixture to a casserole and bake in a slow oven (250 F.) for 1½ hours.

5. Serve on white or brown rice with plain yogurt, a green vegetable and a bottle of dry white wine.

MUSSEL COCKTAIL

Carol Cutler

6 to 8 servings

Even before shrimp prices attained celestial heights, I always preferred serving mussel cocktail to shrimp as the opening course at dinner. The reasons make more sense than ever: 1) price, of course; 2) it is an unexpected presentation; 3) you know you are working with a fresh product since mussels cannot be frozen.

1½ CUPS WATER
1 MEDIUM-SIZED ONION, FINELY CHOPPED
4 OR 5 SPRIGS PARSLEY
1 SMALL BAY LEAF
1 TABLESPOON JUNIPER BERRIES (OPTIONAL, BUT RECOMMENDED)
½ TEASPOON SALT
¼ TEASPOON PEPPER
1 CARROT, FINELY DICED
½ LEMON
3 QUARTS MUSSELS
1 CUP DRY WHITE WINE

LETTUCE FOR LINING SERVING BOWLS

Dressing:
¼ CUP OLIVE OIL
¼ CUP DRY WHITE VERMOUTH
JUICE OF ½ LEMON
¼ TEASPOON CELERY SALT
SALT
PEPPER
¾ CUP MAYONNAISE, PREFERABLY HOMEMADE
¼ CUP CHOPPED PARSLEY

1. In a large pot, combine the water, onion, parsley, bay leaf, juniper berries, salt, pepper, carrot and the lemon half, first squeezing in the juice. Cover and bring to a boil, then simmer for 15 minutes. (This can be done early, and the pot set aside until the final few minutes of cooking.)

2. Carefully scrub the mussels, pulling off all the "beard." Rinse well under cold running water. When ready to cook the mussels, bring the cooked broth back to a boil, add the wine and again bring it to boil.

3. Add the mussels and cover tightly. Keep on high heat and shake the pot once or twice during cooking to mix up the mussels. (If the pot is too large or heavy to shake easily, just stir the mussels quickly with a large spoon.) As soon as the mussels have opened (about five minutes), they are cooked. Remove them from their shells and place them in a mixing bowl.

4. To make the sauce, in a lidded jar combine the olive oil, vermouth, lemon juice, celery salt, salt and pepper and shake vigorously. Pour the dressing over the mussels, toss well and let stand at least 1 hour at room temperature, stirring occasionally.

5. When ready to serve, drain the mussels from the marinade and beat enough of the marinade liquid into the mayonnaise to make a thin sauce. Fold the sauce into the mussels, add the chopped parsley, and heap the mussels into individual lettuce-lined bowls.

Note: For this recipe, the mussels can be cooked the day before serving, removed from their shells and kept in the refrigerator in the strained cooking liquid. Drain off the liquid before proceeding with the recipe.

NEW ORLEANS-STYLE OYSTER
LOAF SANDWICHES

Nan Mabon

Hot Sauce:
1½ CUPS TOMATO CATSUP
2 TABLESPOONS MUSTARD,
   PREFERABLY CREOLE OR USE AN
   IMPORTED MUSTARD SUCH AS
   MOUTARDE DE MEAUX OR
   DIJON-STYLE MUSTARD
2 TABLESPOONS HORSERADISH
2 TABLESPOONS FRESHLY
   SQUEEZED LEMON JUICE
⅛ TEASPOON OR MORE TABASCO
   SAUCE
1 TABLESPOON WORCESTERSHIRE
   SAUCE
SALT
FRESHLY GROUND PEPPER

Other Ingredients:
2 MEDIUM LOAVES FRENCH BREAD,
   UNSLICED
6 TABLESPOONS BUTTER, MELTED
2 DOZEN SHUCKED RAW OYSTERS
½ CUP WHITE CORNMEAL
½ CUP FLOUR
SALT
FRESHLY GROUND PEPPER
PEANUT, VEGETABLE OR CORN
   OIL FOR SHALLOW FRYING
DILL PICKLE SLICES FOR GARNISH
LEMON SLICES FOR GARNISH
FINELY SHREDDED LETTUCE FOR
   GARNISH

1. Combine all of the ingredients for the hot sauce in a mixing bowl, and set the sauce aside.

2. Preheat the oven to 450 F.

3. Cut off the ends of the loaves of the bread and set them aside for another use. Cut the loaves in half, on a slant, across the width, then slice in half lengthwise. This will make four half-loaf sandwiches out of the two loaves. Arrange the quarter loaves, cut side up, on a large baking sheet and brush with melted butter.

4. Drain the oysters.

5. Combine the cornmeal, flour, and some salt and pepper to taste. Blend well. Dredge the oysters, a few at a time, in the cornmeal mixture.

6. Add oil to the skillet to a depth of about ½ inch. Heat the oil until a light haze forms over it. Add half the oysters. When browned on one side, turn and brown on the other. Drain well on absorbent paper. Cook and drain the remaining oysters.

7. Arrange the oysters on the bottom halves of the bread, cover with a top half and wrap each sandwich in foil. Place on a baking sheet in a hot oven and bake about 10 minutes or until warmed through. The bread should not become too crisp. Serve with hot sauce and garnishes.

BELGIAN-STYLE MUSSELS IN CREAM

Florence Fabricant

8 to 10 appetizer servings/4 to 6 main course servings

6 POUNDS MUSSELS
2 CARROTS
2 STALKS CELERY
4 LEEKS (WHITE PART ONLY) OR
  2 MEDIUM-SIZED ONIONS
6 TABLESPOONS BUTTER
1 TEASPOON SALT
½ TEASPOON WHITE PEPPER
2 CUPS DRY WHITE WINE
1 CUP HEAVY CREAM
6 EGG YOLKS
½ TEASPOON LEMON JUICE
2 TABLESPOONS PARSLEY,
  MINCED

1. Scrub the mussels and remove their "beards." Cut the vegetables into match-stick strips about 1-inch long.

2. Melt the butter in a large, heavy casserole. Add the vegetables, salt and pepper and cook over low heat until the vegetables are tender, stirring frequently (about 15 minutes). Do not allow them to brown. Add the wine.

3. Bring the mixture to a boil and add the mussels. Cover and cook until the mussels open (about 10 minutes). While the mussels are cooking, lightly beat the cream with the egg yolks in a bowl.

4. When the mussels have opened (discard any that have not), remove them to a large bowl and cover with a towel to keep warm. Lower the heat under the casserole so the liquid is barely simmering.

5. Add a little of the mussel broth to the cream mixture, stirring with a whisk. Slowly dribble the cream mixture back into the barely simmering broth in the casserole, stirring constantly. Continue cooking the sauce for several minutes, stirring, until it has thickened to the consistency of heavy cream. Do not allow the sauce to simmer or the egg yolks will curdle. Add lemon juice and, if desired, additional salt and pepper.

6. Place the mussels in soup plates. Ladle some of the sauce with the vegetables over the mussels and sprinkle each serving with parsley.

FLAMED DEVILED SHRIMP

Ruth Ellen Church

4 servings

¼ CUP BUTTER
¼ POUND FRESH MUSHROOMS,
  SLICED
1½ POUNDS COOKED, SHELLED
  SHRIMP
2 TABLESPOONS DIJON-STYLE
  MUSTARD
½ TEASPOON SALT
¼ CUP CATSUP
DASH TABASCO OR HOT SAUCE
⅓ CUP BRANDY
1 CUP HEAVY CREAM
2 TABLESPOONS DRY SHERRY OR
  MADEIRA

1. Melt the butter in a pan or chafing dish and add the mushrooms. Sauté for a minute, then add the shrimp, mustard and other seasonings. Heat through.

2. Warm the brandy in a long-handled small pan, ignite it and pour it over the shrimp.

3. When the flames die down, add the cream and heat the sauce through.

4. Stir in sherry or Madeira and serve.

SQUID IN ITS OWN INK WITH GARLIC AND ALMONDS (CALAMARES EN SU TINTA)

Paula Wolfert

8 appetizer servings/4 main course servings

This dish makes an excellent appetizer or main course. When used as a main course, serve with rice.

2 POUNDS SQUID WITH INK SACS
½ CUP WHOLE BLANCHED
  ALMONDS
2 TABLESPOONS CHOPPED
  PARSLEY
7 CLOVES GARLIC, PEELED
2 1-INCH SLICES ITALIAN-STYLE
  BREAD SOAKED IN WATER AND
  SQUEEZED DRY
⅓ CUP OLIVE OIL
2 CUPS DRY WHITE WINE
1 CUP WATER
SALT
FRESHLY GROUND BLACK PEPPER

1. Clean the squid, removing the sac from each head. Set aside the tentacles. Peel off the outer mottled skin and discard the entrails and the thin bone. Put the ink sacs in a sieve. Wash the squid, inside and out, and rinse the tentacles under cold running water; cut them into bite-sized pieces.

2. Chop the almonds, then pound them in a mortar together with the parsley, garlic and bread. Fry this paste in oil in a deep skillet for 2 minutes, stirring. Add the squid, wine and water. Season with salt and pepper. Simmer, covered, stirring occasionally, for 45 minutes.

3. Crush the ink sacs and collect the ink in a bowl. Stir it into the skillet, bring the mixture to a boil, adjust the seasoning and simmer 10 minutes longer. Serve hot.

BAKED SHRIMP ORIENTALE

Emanuel and Madeline Greenberg

8 to 12 appetizer servings/
4 to 6 main course servings

2 POUNDS SHRIMP
⅓ CUP DRY SHERRY
⅓ CUP SOY SAUCE
4 TEASPOONS SALAD OIL
1 LARGE CLOVE GARLIC, CRUSHED
2 TEASPOONS FINELY CHOPPED
 GINGER (OR CANDIED GINGER)
¼ TEASPOON SUGAR (OMIT IF
 USING CANDIED GINGER)
FRESHLY GROUND PEPPER, TO
 TASTE

1. Slit the shrimp up the back and rinse out the sand vein. Do not remove the shells.

2. Pour the sherry and soy sauce into a measuring cup and add salad oil up to the ¾ cup mark. Stir in the remaining ingredients.

3. Pour the mixture over the shrimp and marinate for about 2 hours, turning occasionally.

4. Arrange the shrimp in a single layer in a shallow baking pan. Pour the marinade over them.

5. Bake in a preheated 400 F. oven for 8 minutes.

BAKED LOBSTER

Julie Dannenbaum

1 serving

This is my favorite method of preparing lobster. The method was taught to me many years ago by a fisherman on the New Jersey shore.

1 LOBSTER WEIGHING 1½ POUNDS
6 TABLESPOONS BUTTER, CUT INTO
  CHIPS
½ LEMON
EXTRA MELTED BUTTER AND
  LEMON WEDGES FOR SERVING

1. Split the live lobster lengthwise, head to tail, or have your fish market do it. Remove the sac behind the eyes along with the spinal cord.

2. Lay the split lobster on a baking sheet and distribute chipped butter over it.

3. Squeeze the juice of half a lemon over the lobster.

4. Place in a preheated 350 F. oven and bake 20 to 30 minutes, or until the lobster turns red. Do not overcook. Serve the lobster with extra melted butter and lemon wedges.

SCALLOPS IN DILLED WINE SAUCE

Julie Dannenbaum

4 appetizer servings/2 to 3 main course servings

An elegant diet dish, low in calories, not at all rich but most appealing.

1 POUND BAY SCALLOPS
¾ CUP DRY WHITE WINE
½ CUP FINELY CHOPPED
  SHALLOTS
2 EGG YOLKS
1 TABLESPOON FINELY CHOPPED
  FRESH DILL
½ MEDIUM-SIZED TOMATO, VERY
  RIPE, PEELED, CHOPPED AND
  SEEDED
SALT
FRESHLY GROUND WHITE PEPPER

1. Put the scallops into a sauté pan and toss them over medium-high heat for 3 to 4 minutes. No fat is needed in the pan because the scallops will give off their liquid.

2. Remove the scallops from the pan and set them aside. Reserve the liquid left in the pan.

3. Place the shallots and wine in a small, heavy pan and reduce the wine to 3 tablespoons over medium heat.

4. Whisk the egg yolks in a small, heavy pan with 2 tablespoons of the cooled wine-shallot reduction. Do this over medium heat, whisking until the mixture mounds.

5. When thick and frothy, add the remaining shallot mixture to the egg yolk mixture. Then add the reserved scallop juice, dill, tomato, salt and pepper. Mix thoroughly.

6. Combine the sauce with the scallops and set over low heat for a few minutes to reheat the scallops.

SWEET RED PEPPER AND LOBSTER STEW

Elizabeth Colchie

4 servings

1 3-POUND LOBSTER
  (APPROXIMATELY)
2 CUPS SWEET RED PEPPER,
  CHOPPED
¼ CUP OLIVE OIL
1 TEASPOON MINCED GARLIC
1 TEASPOON COARSE SALT
1 TEASPOON POWDERED FENNEL
¼ TEASPOON SAFFRON
4 TEASPOONS FLOUR
1 CUP WATER
1 CUP DRY WHITE WINE
LEMON JUICE
PEPPER

1. Steam (or boil) the lobster for about 20 minutes. Cool. Remove the meat, slice it, and place it in a bowl with the juices, roe and tomalley. Set aside.

2. In a skillet, sauté the pepper in olive oil until softened, about 10 minutes.

3. In a mortar, crush together the garlic, salt, fennel and saffron and stir the mixture into the peppers. Sauté for a minute or two.

4. Sprinkle flour into the skillet and stir for a few minutes.

5. Add the water and wine and bring to a simmer, stirring. Simmer for about 10 minutes, stirring often.

6. Add the lobster, cook over low heat and stir until it is heated through. Season with lemon juice and pepper.

MEXICAN SEAFOOD APPETIZER

Diana Kennedy

4 servings

2 DOZEN LARGE, RAW CLAMS, OR
  SUBSTITUTE SCALLOPS OR
  MEDIUM-SIZED COOKED SHRIMP
1 LARGE TOMATO, UNSKINNED
3 FRESH, HOT GREEN CHILIES, OR
  TO TASTE
1 SMALL ONION
⅓ CUP FRESH LIME JUICE
1 MEDIUM-SIZED AVOCADO
CHOPPED CORIANDER LEAVES
  (*CILANTRO*) (OPTIONAL)
SALT
3 TABLESPOONS OLIVE OIL

1. If you are using clams, remove them from their shells, reserving the juice.

2. Finely chop the tomato, chilies and onion.

3. Peel the avocado and chop the flesh into ½-inch squares.

4. Mix the clams and their juice, or the scallops or shrimp, if you are using them, with the rest of the ingredients and set aside for the flavors to marry for about 20 minutes.

5. Serve cold, but not so cold that the oil congeals.

SEVICHE ORIENTALE

Michael Batterberry

8 hors d'oeuvre servings / 4 first course servings

½ POUND FILLET OF GRAY SOLE
½ POUND SMALL BAY SCALLOPS
⅔ CUP LIME JUICE
4 SCALLIONS, FINELY SLICED
  (WITH ½ THEIR GREEN ENDS)
1½ TEASPOONS GRATED FRESH
  GINGER
1 TEASPOON DARK SESAME OIL
1 TABLESPOON SALAD OIL
CHINESE HOT OIL OR TABASCO
PINCH OF SUGAR

1. Cut the sole into large postage stamp-sized pieces, being careful to remove any lingering spinal tissue.

2. Combine the sole, bay scallops (cut in half crosswise if on the large side), lime juice and scallions. Toss lightly and refrigerate for 4 to 6 hours, tossing

several times during this period to be sure lime juice "cooks" the seafood evenly.

3. Drain off all the juices and dress with the sauce made by whisking together the ginger, sesame and salad oils, the pinch of sugar and as much hot oil or Tabasco as suits you—flavor should be more warm than fiery.

4. Refrigerate until ice cold and serve. For an appetizer, serve with wooden picks. For a first course, arrange the *seviche* on individual plates on top of little mounds of finely shredded lettuce hearts dressed with a trace of peanut or corn oil.

CHERRYSTONE CLAMS SIMMERED IN WHITE WINE WITH SHALLOTS

Paul Rubinstein

4 appetizer servings

8 TABLESPOONS (1 STICK) BUTTER
3 TABLESPOONS FRESH OR
  FROZEN CHOPPED SHALLOTS
2 TABLESPOONS FRESH OR
  FROZEN CHOPPED CHIVES
1 CUP DRY WHITE WINE
1 TABLESPOON LEMON JUICE
1 TEASPOON FRESHLY GROUND
  WHITE PEPPER
24 CHERRYSTONE CLAMS ON THE
  HALF SHELL

1. In a large skillet or other shallow pan equipped with a cover, melt the butter over low heat. Add the shallots and cook 2 or 3 minutes until they soften.

2. Add the chives, wine, lemon juice and pepper, then place the clams, in their half shells, in the liquid. The pan should be large enough so that all the clams can fit in a single layer.

3. Cover the pan and simmer 10 minutes over medium heat.

4. To serve, place portions of 6 clams per person on individual plates, spoon some liquid from the pan over them and serve hot.

EDITORS

Arnold Goldman
Barbara Spiegel
Lyn Stallworth

EDITORIAL ASSISTANT

Christopher Carter

EDITORIAL CONSULTANTS

Wendy Afton Rieder
Kate Slate

CONTRIBUTORS

Introduction by Irene Sax

Michael Batterberry, author of several books on food, art and social history, is also a painter, editor and food critic for several national magazines. He has taught at James Beard's cooking classes in New York and many of his original recipes have appeared in *House & Garden, House Beautiful* and *Harper's Bazaar.*

Paula J. Buchholz is the regional co-ordinator for the National Culinary Apprenticeship Program. She has been a food writer for the *Detroit Free Press* and for the *San Francisco Examiner.*

Giuliano Bugialli, author of *The Fine Art of Italian Cooking,* is co-founder and teacher of Cooking in Florence, a program conducted in Italy. He also has a cooking school in New York.

Vilma Liacouras Chantiles, author of *The Food of Greece,* writes a food and consumer column for the *Scarsdale* (New York) *Inquirer* and a monthly food column for the *Athenian Magazine* (Athens, Greece).

Ruth Ellen Church, a syndicated wine columnist for the *Chicago Tribune,* had been food editor for that newspaper for more than thirty years when she recently retired. The author of seven cookbooks, her most recent book is *Entertaining with Wine.* Mrs. Church's *Wines and Cheeses of the Midwest* will be published in the fall of 1977.

Elizabeth Colchie is a noted food consultant who has done extensive recipe development and testing as well as research into the history of foods and cookery. She was on the editorial staff of *The Cooks' Catalogue* and has written numerous articles for such magazines as *Gourmet, House & Garden* and *Family Circle.*

Carol Cutler, who has been a food columnist for the *Washington Post,* is a graduate of the Cordon Bleu and L'Ecole des Trois Gourmands in Paris. She is the author of *Haute Cuisine for Your Heart's Delight* and *The Six-Minute Soufflé and Other Culinary Delights.* She has also written for *House & Garden, American Home* and *Harper's Bazaar.*

Julie Dannenbaum is the founding director of the largest non-professional cooking school in the country, the Creative Cooking School in Philadelphia. She is the author of *Julie Dannenbaum's Creative Cooking School* and *Menus for All Occasions.* She is also Director of the Gritti Palace Hotel Cooking School in Venice and The Grand Hotel Cooking School in Rome.

Nathalie Dupree has been Director of Rich's Cooking School in Atlanta, Georgia, since it opened in September, 1975. She has an Advanced Certificate from the London Cordon Bleu and has owned restaurants in Spain and Georgia.

Florence Fabricant is a free-lance writer, reporting on restaurants and food for *The New York Times, New York* magazine and other publications. She was on the staff of *The Cooks' Catalogue* and was editor of the paperback edition.

Emanuel and Madeline Greenberg co-authored *Whiskey in the Kitchen* and are consultants to the food and beverage industry. Emanuel, a home economist, is a regular contributor to the food columns of *Playboy* magazine.

Diana Kennedy, the leading authority on the food of Mexico, is the author of *The Cuisines of Mexico* and *The Tortilla Book.*

Carole Lalli is a contributing editor to *New West* magazine and its restaurant reviewer. She formerly ran a catering business in New York.

Jeanne Lesem, Family Editor of United Press International, is the author of *The Pleasures of Preserving and Pickling.*

Nan Mabon, a free-lance food writer and cooking teacher in New York City, is also the cook for a private executive dining room on Wall Street. She studied at the Cordon Bleu in London.

Helen McCully is food editor of *House Beautiful* magazine and the author of many books on food, among them *Nobody Ever Tells You These Things About Food and Drink, Cooking with Helen McCully Beside You,* and most recently, *Waste Not, Want Not: A Cookbook of Delicious Foods from Leftovers.* She was a consultant on the staff of *The Cooks' Catalogue.*

Gloria Bley Miller is the author of *Learn Chinese Cooking in Your Own Kitchen* and *The Thousand Recipe Chinese Cookbook.*

Maurice Moore-Betty, owner-operator of The Civilized Art Cooking School, food consultant and restaurateur, is author of *Cooking for Occasions, The Maurice Moore-Betty Cooking School Book of Fine Cooking* and *The Civilized Art of Salad Making.*

Toshio Morimoto is the owner of Kitcho, a highly regarded Japanese restaurant in New York City. He was the consulting chef for the *Cooking of Japan* in Time-Life Books' *Foods of the World* Series.

Jane Moulton, a food writer for the *Plain Dealer* in Cleveland, took her degree in foods and nutrition. As well as reporting on culinary matters and reviewing food-related books for the *Plain Dealer,* she has worked in recipe development, public relations and catering.

Paul Rubinstein is the author of *Feasts for Two, The Night Before Cookbook* and *Feasts for Twelve (or More).* He is a stockbroker and the son of pianist Artur Rubinstein.

Raymond Sokolov, author of *The Saucier's Apprentice,* is a free-lance writer with a particular interest in food.

Harvey Steiman is food editor of the *Miami Herald.* He has taught cooking classes and lectured on wine and restaurants at the Food and Hotel School of Florida International University.

Joanne Will is food editor of the *Chicago Tribune* and a member of three Chicago wine and food societies.

Paula Wolfert, author of *Mediterranean Cooking* and *Couscous and Other Good Food from Morocco,* is also a cooking teacher and consultant. She has written articles for *Vogue* and other magazines.

Nicola Zanghi is the owner-chef of Restaurant Zanghi in Glen Cove, New York. He started his apprenticeship under his father at the age of thirteen, and is a graduate of two culinary colleges. He has been an instructor at Anna Muffoletto's Cordon Bleu school in New York City.